Napoleon's Last Will and Testament

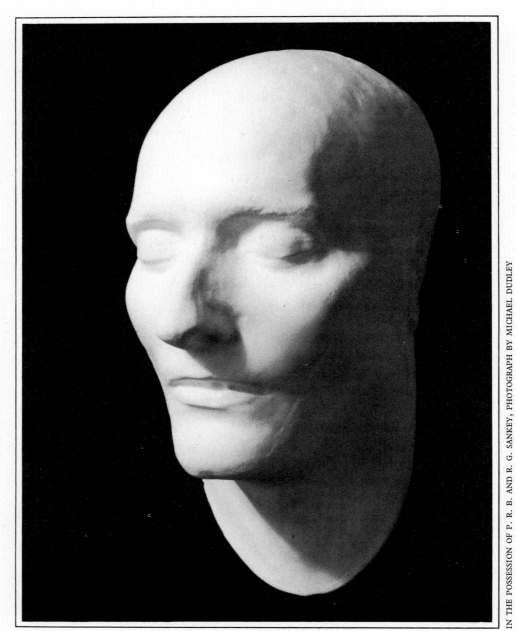

Napoleon's death mask

Napoleon's Last Will and Testament

A facsimile edition of the original document, together with its codicils, appended inventories, letters and instructions, preserved in the French National Archives

Commentaries by
JEAN-PIERRE BABELON
Curator of the Museum of French History
and
SUZANNE D'HUART
Curator of the French National Archives
Translated from the French and introduced by
ALEX de JONGE

PADDINGTON PRESS LTD
NEW YORK & LONDON

Library of Congress Cataloging in Publication Data

Napoléon I, Emperor of the French, 1769-1821.
Napoléon's last will and testament.

1. Napoléon I, Emperor of the French, 1769-1821
--Will. I. Title.
DC214.3.N3613   944.06'092'4 [B]   77-6665
ISBN 0-448-22190-X
ISBN 0-448-22186-1 pbk.

Published by arrangement with Club du Livre, Paris, France
French edition © 1969 Club du Livre

English-language edition © 1977 Paddington Press (U.K.) Limited
All rights reserved

Filmset in England by SX Composing Ltd., Leigh-on-Sea, Essex
Printed in England by Balding & Mansell Ltd., Wisbech, Cambs.

Designed by Richard Johnson
Picture research by Enid Moore
ENDPAPERS: Longwood, Napoleon's home on St. Helena

IN THE UNITED STATES
PADDINGTON PRESS LTD.
Distributed by
GROSSET & DUNLAP

IN THE UNITED KINGDOM
PADDINGTON PRESS LTD.

IN CANADA
Distributed by
RANDOM HOUSE OF CANADA LTD.

IN AUSTRALIA
Distributed by
ANGUS & ROBERTSON PTY. LTD.

IN SOUTHERN AFRICA
Distributed by
ERNEST STANTON (PUBLISHERS) (PTY.) LTD.

Contents

Introduction

"WHAT A ROMANCE my life has been," Napoleon once said reflectively, in exile on the island of St. Helena. The remark is typical; it combines a peculiar detachment, which permitted him to see an overall picture where lesser men would get bogged down in detail, with another quality no less important—the sense that he was an adventurer, and that his life, notwithstanding the pomp and circumstance of a coronation by the pope, his mastery of most of Europe and his marriage into one of Europe's oldest dynasties, was itself no more than an adventure, a series of tides taken at the flood. Napoleon was no Alexander, born to a kingdom which he made into an empire. He was merely a genius who availed himself unaided of a unique combination of circumstance and luck. As he put it himself, centuries would pass before the pattern of events which led to his career recurred in the case of another. One wonders whether Hitler would have agreed with him. Napoleon's achievement, viewed objectively, defies consideration. It is the greatest success story of modern history, a story which was to haunt generations of restless young men who would measure their achievements against those of Buonaparte and find their own sadly wanting. His legend would generate a whole new idiom of success or failure stories, tales of would-be empire-builders and "superior beings," creating fictional characters as diverse as Stendhal's Julien Sorel, Dostoevsky's Raskolnikov and Welles's Citizen Kane.

Napoleon himself was not of humble origins. He was born in Ajaccio, Corsica, on August 15, 1769, and his father was of noble birth, a leading citizen of his town, and the descendant of a noble Florentine family which could be traced back to the eleventh century. Although in later years he would turn his back upon his Corsican beginnings he was marked by it in some respects. He displayed great loyalty to his family and to old comrades, to the extent of giving jobs to the boys which the boys could not always handle. Loyalty emerges also in his will, where he is anxious to reward those who have served him well, to set up marriages, create family alliances. He is moreover quite capable of being extremely vindictive. All these might be considered "Corsican" qualities. Yet more important, perhaps, was the detachment he derived from his non-French background. It enabled him, from the outset, to stand back from French affairs and view them objectively, and this objectivity was the foundation of his strategic and political genius. Furthermore, although he may have had the overreaching ambitions of a Tamburlaine he lacked that petty vanity that has marked so many French political figures from Louis XIV to de Gaulle. He was an altogether bigger man.

Napoleon was born the year following Genoa's sale of Corsica to France. His father was a supporter of an anti-French resistance movement led by General Paoli. When he was defeated Charles Buonaparte accepted French rule and the governor of Corsica obtained for his second son Napoleon a scholarship at a school for the sons of nobles at Brienne.

It would seem that he worked hard, and was somewhat teased by his fellow pupils for his strange accent. He showed great ability in mathematics, and in 1784 was given a place at the École Militaire, the West Point of France, where he distinguished himself by passing out in one year as opposed to three and graduating high on the list. He was immediately commissioned as a lieutenant in an artillery regiment. Artillery has always been the "thinking soldier's" arm, and never more so than during the latter part of the eighteenth century. Great advances had been made in the technology of cannon design and in strategic theory, advances which Napoleon was to build on in the evolution of his own theories of war: concentrate your men, concentrate your guns, move fast and hit the enemy hard in one place, preferably a flank.

Napoleon's first posting, to Auxonne, was in 1789, the year of the French Revolution. He played little part in it at first. He went over to the nation from the crown with no qualms. Revolution for him meant Corsican independence. He returned to his island, raised the standard of revolution and secured a promise from the new government that Corsicans would henceforward be considered full French citizens. Paoli returned from exile to be greeted as a liberator. However, Corsican affairs grew confused, and rough, providing Napoleon with his political initiation. Paoli went over to the royalist and clerical faction which sought to dissociate Corsica from revolutionary France. Napoleon, who had obtained election to a volunteer battalion by kidnapping the opposition, and had subsequently ordered his men to fire on pro-religious rioters, was denounced by Paoli's side. He had moreover failed to report as ordered to his regiment, and had been struck off the army list. In the circumstances he felt it urgent that he return to Paris.

Fortunately for Napoleon, war had broken out with Austria and he was both reinstated and promoted to captain. In September 1792 he returned to Corsica to fetch his sister Elisa back to France. He was never to visit the island again, being, as he would say, preoccupied with "more important things."

In the summer of 1793 republican France had declared ideological war on the traditional monarchies of Europe, and half her departments were in the grips of civil war. Toulon, one of her most important naval bases, had welcomed the English and Spanish fleets. It was besieged by the revolutionary general Carteaux, under whom Napoleon was serving. His luck now began to work for him. Within two days of the siege the artillery commander was wounded and Napoleon took over. He saw that the key to the siege was a fort dominating the harbour, but was unable to seize it at once. He eventually got a free hand in the deployment of his guns and in due course the fort fell and the English felt obliged to leave. It was clear to all that the success of the siege was largely thanks to Napoleon. His general congratulated him for his skill and courage, while Robespierre's brother found him "an artillery officer of transcendent merit." He had been lucky, it is true, that circumstances had allowed him to play his own hand, but he had played it immaculately.

His career now underwent a momentary eclipse, and it took a political crisis to bring him back to the forefront of events. The infamous "Reign of Terror," established by the National Convention in response to the needs of strong internal government and a vigorous war policy, came to an end with the fall and execution of Robespierre. His dictatorship was replaced by a Directory of five men, but its career was stormy. There was an increasingly powerful royalist faction asserting itself in Paris.

In the autumn of 1795 the population of the capital was suffering from famine, falling currency, rising prices and war-weariness. The National Convention nearly provoked its own overthrow by advocating a constitution designed to ensure that it remained in power. It appointed Barras, who had been at Toulon, to take charge of the armed forces. He picked Napoleon as his second in command. There was a fire fight at the Tuileries during which Napoleon lost thirty men, and the enemy lost a great deal more by virtue of his famous "whiff of grapeshot." Napoleon had his priorities right. In his view it was pointless to try to quell a mob by firing blanks: "They are frightened at first but soon come back when they see that there are no casualties, and then you have to kill them in large quantities. One volley of ball killing a few is much more effective." As usual the desire to get results overrode his scruples. Napoleon was rewarded by promotion to the rank of major-general and eventual command of the army of the interior. He was twenty-six years old.

It was at this time that he began his courtship of Joséphine de Beauharnais, a beautiful thirty-two-year-old créole whose husband had been killed in the Terror. She first became his mistress and then his wife. They were married on March 9, 1796. It would seem that Napoleon wanted a marriage and there is much evidence to suppose that he loved her. She at least wanted security. The fact that she was subsequently consistently unfaithful to him does not mean that she did not find him attractive. Her name was on his lips when he died.

Two days after his wedding Napoleon was given command of the army of Italy, and there began that miraculous celebration of youth, energy and success which set the tone of his early and triumphant years. His appointment made him alter his name from Buono- to Bonaparte.

He now began the series of victories that made him. From the start he displayed an extraordinary capacity for detailed planning; the study of his opponent's dispositions, psychology, the terrain, the weather. He believed that every battle had its potential turning point, the moment when one additional piece of pressure properly applied would make the difference between defeat and victory. It was his vision, his sense of what to look for and when to take his opportunities which ensured that this turning point was usually found.

Napoleon led a tiny army of thirty thousand starving, bare-foot, ill-equipped men into the fertile plains of Italy. Through a series of brilliant battles he delivered the whole of northern Italy to France. Not only was he able to pay his troops, he could actually send money back to his government. Already he was thinking in terms of a grand strategy, concerned not just with the Italian campaign against the Austrians but with the effect which this would have upon Austrian troops on the Rhine frontier. Already his correspondence shows him seeing the whole of Europe spread before him as one campaign map. Napoleon won some twelve victories in as many months, even though some of them, such as Arcola, were expensive. The campaign against Austria resulted in the Treaty of Campo Formio, which guaranteed France both Belgium and the left bank of the Rhine. Already a successful general, Napoleon was virtually independent of his government, free to name his own terms and negotiate on his own behalf.

Young as he was his contemporaries saw him as a man of destiny. One general described him as "the sort of man of whom nature is sparing and who only appears on earth at intervals of centuries." He himself believed that he was "destined to change the face of the world."

It may have been this belief which explains his next ambition, the eventual conquest of India—to which he believed Egypt to be the key. More by luck than by judgment Napoleon's convoy to Egypt, which included a collection of scholars and orientalists, landed there unchallenged despite the fact that Nelson was cruising the Mediterranean looking for it. Napoleon captured Alexandria within hours of landing, on July 2, 1798, and advanced across the desert toward Cairo. He routed the Egyptian army at the Battle of the Pyramids with the loss of only thirty men, and on July 14 he entered Cairo. However, his successes were negated by the total loss of his fleet at Nelson's hands at the Battle of Aboukir Bay on August 1. Napoleon tried to achieve a political victory in Egypt, seeking to persuade the Egyptians that the French were not simply infidel invaders. As always, a political sense supported his military genius and he realized that winning battles was not enough. He showed great respect for the traditions of Islam and sought to get the French accepted as liberators. Yet, as was often the case, his understanding of the need for a political solution was inhibited by his belief that such solutions could be effected with the speed of military maneuvers. He subsequently attempted to extend his sphere of influence in the Middle East, but failed to conquer Syria. Although he defeated a massive Turkish invasion force at the battle of Alexandria, this failed to consolidate his long-term position. When on August 21, 1799, he learnt that Italy had been lost and French armies defeated on the Rhine he felt that Europe needed him. He abandoned his own army and sailed for France in the greatest secrecy.

He landed at Fréjus on October 8 to be hailed as the savior of the republic, the only man who could prevent the restoration of the monarchy. It was on this basis that he planned the *coup d'état* of 18 Brumaire, November 9, 1799. He did not present himself as a candidate— he was chosen; the members of the Directory of five looked to him to assume or support a dictatorship. The *coup d'état* did not go off entirely smoothly: there was a moment when Napoleon made an inept speech to the Jacobin lower house, and was nearly lynched. His brother Lucien, president of the assembly, saved the day and brought in troops to protect him. That evening Bonaparte, and two associates, Sieyès and Ducros, were elected Consuls.

The Directory of five had been replaced by a Consulate of three and the three were almost immediately replaced by one. Napoleon had understood the lines of force, the currents of power, which obtained at the time, and this clarity of vision brought him to power where a lesser adventurer might, literally, have lost his head. The French wanted powerful, stable and positive rule, but did not want a Bourbon restoration. The time was ripe for them to accept centralized institutions and virtual dictatorship. Almost at once Napoleon became the only consul, elected for a term of ten years. He used his new powers to reform the country's administrative and fiscal structures, eliminating decentralized institutions and providing a highly centralized pattern of government, that of the *préfet* and *sous-préfet* who have administered France through the nine different kinds of leadership it has enjoyed ever since. He also instituted a Council of State, drawn from the ablest men in the country regardless of their politics. He was only interested in assembling talent, and in the Council of State he created the most talented, hard-working and able body of men that France had ever known. It was the reforms of the Consulate which formed the basis for the triumphs of the Empire, and which, indeed, created the political structure of modern France.

Napoleon had offered peace terms to Austria and England on December 25, 1799, but was only prepared to negotiate on the basis of the Treaty of Campo Formio, a basis which

Austria declined. In order to keep his opponents guessing Napoleon massed his reserve army at Dijon. From there he could strike at Italy or the Rhine. In fact he had plans for both fronts, again displaying a sense of overall strategy. His Rhine army would attack under General Moreau, while his Italian army under Masséna would keep the Austrians in play. In the meantime he would come through the Alpine passes and take the Austrians in the rear. He saw the whole front from Genoa to the Danube as a single pattern, and it is this sense of strategy combined with an infinite capacity for detail, without one order of thought ever inhibiting the other, that characterizes his particular genius.

The campaign was only partially successful until Napoleon faced the Austrians at Marengo on June 14, 1800. It was in fact a battle that he nearly lost, and to lose it would have been to lose everything. It was only an unexpected counterattack with a division of fresh troops that enabled Napoleon to shatter an Austrian army which believed that it had already won the day. It was a fascinating fight and one that stretched the young commander to his limit. He had exploited chance, the fluidity of battle and rapidity of movement to the full, and, once more, luck, together with judgment and self-confidence, had swung the balance for him. It was a very Napoleonic kind of victory, and one which was to consolidate his by no means unshakable political position.

Napoleon's political acumen can be seen in his policy toward the Catholic church. He instinctively sensed the important hold religion had over simple minds and sought to make peace with the pope, dissociating himself from the antireligious policies of the Revolution. The result was the so-called Concordat of 1801, which recognized the Catholic religion and the right to worship. Although it did not entirely satisfy the pope from the outset, it went a long way to repairing the damage done by the anticlericalism of the Revolution.

He assisted the political consolidation of his powers by the institution of the Légion d'Honneur. The old orders of chivalry had of course been abolished by the Revolution, but Napoleon understood enough of his nation to appreciate that one way of strengthening his regime was to reward sentiments of honor and vanity with decorations and titles. These he reconciled with his famous idea of a society open to all talents. He again reveals his profound understanding of the vanity and the egocentricity of the French. "The French are unable to desire anything seriously except, perhaps, equality. Even so they would gladly renounce it if everyone could entertain the hope of rising to the top. Equality in the sense that everyone will be the master; there you have the secret of all your vanities. What must be done therefore is to give everybody the hope of being able to rise." Here as always he was aware of the need to create institutions and habits of thought which would help to consolidate his own position as a military dictator, with no divine right, no pattern of hereditary authority to support him. It was this same sense of priorities which, while he always remained tolerant of private criticism, made him reject, absolutely, any form of public opposition. He knew that he could not afford it. Thus he set up the most rigorous censorship of the press and control of public opinion. He felt that with a free press he "would not remain three days in power."

In 1802 he signed the Peace of Amiens with the English. Although this could only be a truce many people in France saw it as the end to a decade of war, and Napoleon's popularity grew to new heights. A vote of gratitude was proposed and a plebiscite made Napoleon Consul for life, with the right of nominating his own successor—a situation tantamount to the restoration of a hereditary monarchy. The life consulate gave Napoleon far more power than any French monarch had enjoyed hitherto. Absolute power vested in one person, centralization, equality and the abolition of hereditary privilege; these, Napoleon could see, were the true aims of the Revolution. A decade of flirtation with democratic and decentralized institutions had obscured the fact to most eyes, and accordingly Napoleon was accused of having betrayed the Revolution. In fact he was simply realizing its true objectives and giving the French people the kind of government which they had been conditioned to want—and would continue to want for the next hundred and fifty years.

During this period there were numerous plots against Napoleon's life, royalist, and in some cases English-inspired. Napoleon's chief of police, the great Fouché, provided him with information suggesting that one such plot was to be headed by a Bourbon prince already in Europe. Suspicion fell on the Duke of Enghien, who was living in the Duchy of Baden, just across the Rhine. Napoleon had him kidnapped, brought to Paris, and shot after a summary trial. It was an action which did his reputation great damage abroad. Beethoven removed the dedication of the Eroica Symphony to him, observing that Napoleon was no more than a mere man who would in time become a tyrant. Nevertheless the execution of a Bourbon did much to reconcile Napoleon to republican elements at home, and in his will he states that he does not regret his action (see pages 38–9).

The threats to his life encouraged him to consolidate his position by making it hereditary. On December 2, 1804, Napoleon received the imperial crown from the hands of the pope himself in Notre Dame cathedral, and placed it upon his own head. He had arranged for his old nurse to attend the ceremony, and shortly beforehand had been heard to observe to his brother Joseph: "If only our father could see us now"—once again something of the adventurer comes through the imperial image.

Napoleon, although himself a man of simple tastes, was fully aware that his empire lacked foundations, and sought to compensate for that lack through pomp and circumstance. He accepted that an emperor could have no private life, and submitted himself to ceremonials even more elaborate than those of the Bourbon court. He also ensured that his empire would have an image, a style, with its pseudo-Renaissance robes, the imperial banner with its bees, and the echoes of imperial Rome in the decorative art of his age.

"Kingship is an actor's part," he observed, and he was prepared to carry the act to any lengths in order to consolidate his power base. He was even prepared to reintroduce the notion of a hereditary nobility—a reward for outstanding service, supported by grants of land. Although the traditional French aristocracy have never taken the *Noblesse d'Empire* seriously there is no doubt that Napoleon's step made his position as the would-be founder of a dynasty that much more secure. His actions have been presented as those of a *parvenu* seeking to outdo traditional aristocratic castes—and yet this is not so. He was, rather, motivated by his sense of the long-term strategies necessary for the continuation of his dynasty, and a loyal aristocracy raised to its rank by his favor was a necessary ingredient. At the same time he would always state that he did not need the praise or the admiration of smart Parisians; only the opinions of the "well-off peasant" concerned him. However, he went to great lengths to ensure that the Parisian working class was fully employed and well fed. The Revolution had taught him the lesson that he who holds Paris holds France, and that a hungry mob could shift the balance of power in a matter of hours. For all the pomp and apparent vanity of his court, he never lost his grasp on the essentials of power, and if his ceremonials and his rewards pandered to greed and vanity then it was to the vanity of his subjects, and not to his own, that they addressed themselves. The Légion d'Honneur after all is an institution that has stood the test of time remarkably well.

The Empire was an attempt to unite Revolutionary and pre-Revolutionary France, and in due course many old émigré families "rallied" to it. Napoleon's internal position seemed secure enough, but he realized that he could never be completely safe until England was defeated. The Peace of Amiens broke down in May 1803, and by the next year Napoleon had massed a great invasion army at Boulogne. Yet in order to invade England he had to have control of the Channel, if only for twenty-four hours. Napoleon was reluctant to admit that the French navy was significantly inferior to the British, and unable to accept that it would take years to make up its deficiencies. Temperamentally unsympathetic to "long-haul" military solutions, he later admitted that he never really understood naval affairs, and that this lack of understanding blocked all his ideas on the subject.

Napoleon's attempt to gain temporary mastery of the Channel straits failed. Villeneuve, his admiral, found himself bottled up in Cadiz by the English fleet. Napoleon abandoned invasion plans and ordered his Boulogne army to break camp. Villeneuve attempted to break the Cadiz blockade on October 21, 1805, only to have his fleet annihilated at the Battle of Trafalgar, thereby ensuring British naval superiority for the rest of the Napoleonic era.

The great powers, England, Austria, Prussia, Russia, were as suspicious of one another as they were of Napoleon. He had been able to maintain Prussian neutrality by offering her Hanover and control of northern Germany. Austria had been exhausted by her wars with France. Alexander of Russia was an indecisive and weak young man who had no clear political vision, simply certain unfocused ambitions. However, English diplomacy and Napoleon's ambitious plans for control of the Near East began to turn the tsar against him. The next, Third, coalition against Napoleon was sparked off by his proposal to change Italy from a republic into a hereditary kingdom. He was crowned King of all Italy in Milan in May 1805. In the meantime an Anglo-Russian treaty had been signed and joined by the Austrians. Prussia preferred to wait.

It was assumed that the fighting would take place in Italy. Archduke Charles commanded the main Austrian army in Venetia and the Tyrol. He was held off by Masséna with an army of some 40,000 men while Napoleon moved from Boulogne with remarkable speed to put over 200,000 men across the Rhine within six weeks of setting out. Mack, the Austrian commander, was totally unprepared, and was forced to surrender his army of 50,000 at Ulm. The Russian commander Kutuzov now had control over the joint Austrian and Russian forces. He fought a brilliant withdrawal action, though it required him to hand Vienna over to the French. Yet at this stage, as Prussia became increasingly inclined to war with France, things began to look bad for Napoleon. It was essential that he destroy the Austrians and Russians before the Prussians joined them. To wipe out individual armies before they could unite was always a prime objective. However, Kutuzov refused to be drawn into battle. Fortunately for Napoleon, Tsar Alexander now arrived at the front in person. Listening to appallingly bad advice from influential but incompetent staff officers he decided to stand and fight, using a battle plan which left Kutuzov in silent despair. The allied army made its stand at Austerlitz on December 2, 1805. Badly coordinated, it over-extended itself in order to try to outflank the French left. This was just the sort of tactic which invited a concentrated attack from Napoleon. He saw and seized his opportunity, mounting a massed attack on the allied center and cutting their armies in two to win the greatest of all his victories with the greatest of all his armies, the *grande armée* at its highest point. It was an army which, granted its commander, was virtually invincible. News of the shattering defeat of Austerlitz impelled Austria to make a separate peace with France, the Treaty of Pressburg. Prussia also quickly signed a treaty with Napoleon.

Yet peace did not last long. By her new treaty Prussia had been given Hanover, and Napoleon was perfectly content to allow her to maintain her control over northern Germany. However, in the meantime he sought to put his brother Joseph on the throne of Sicily. The Bourbon ruler, Ferdinand, was to receive the Balearic Isles in compensation. England reluctantly agreed these terms, securing Hanover's reversion to the English crown in compensation. She then proceeded to inform the Prussians that the reversion of Hanover was to be the price of a continuing peace. This was enough to make Frederick William of Prussia decide to declare war on the French on October 7, 1806. He had the support of Russia and Saxony.

The Prussian army still enjoyed the reputation made for it by Frederick the Great—a reputation which was to remain with it for one short week. Frederick's tactics were rigid and slow, the army had massive baggage trains and inexperienced officers. They proved quite incapable of coping with Napoleon's tactics of rapid deployment and mobility when the two armies met at Jena on October 14, 1806. The Prussians lost some 45,000 men and all their artillery. Ten days later the French entered Berlin and by November 6 peace terms were agreed.

Napoleon was moving steadily east. Promising or half-promising Polish patriots liberation and independence from Russia, he began to test the strength of the Russian army early in 1807. His efforts were inconclusive and culminated in the terrible Battle of Eylau, February 8, 1807, where, as would later prove the case at Borodino, Russians and French both stood their ground to produce an inconclusive battle with severe casualties on both sides.

Napoleon was not in the strongest of positions. Austria appeared to threaten his right flank, although she was reluctant to tackle him again so soon after Austerlitz. His army was increased by conscripts, but it was no longer the superb fighting force it had been only two years before. However, England was in no hurry to send troops to assist her Russian and Prussian allies, and these were beginning to lose heart. The process was completed by the Battle of Friedland, a characteristic Napoleonic victory, and one worth looking at in more detail.

The Russian forces were commanded by Bennigsen, the architect of Austerlitz, who confirmed his military incompetence on June 14, 1807. Having given the French something of a bloody nose at Helsberg, and then withdrawing in such a way that he lost contact for three days, Bennigsen, thinking he was faced only with a light advance guard, moved his whole army across the Alle river, which confined his line of retreat to a mere handful of bridges. The French advance guard under Marshal Lannes held off the Russians, while Napoleon brought up his army. He arrived at noon, and was able to deploy some 40,000 men. He launched an attack on the Russian left where they were crowded onto a narrow tongue of land between the river and a millstream. He used a heavy artillery bombardment to soften them up and then Marshal Ney began to push the Russians toward Friedland itself, reaching the river and rolling them up. The Russian army was pushed and huddled against the river bends. Then the French cavalry drove the Russian horse back against its own infantry along the river, while the artillery advanced *en masse* to within case-shot range to inflict the first massive artillery bombardment in history. The Russian defence collapsed within minutes and their losses were terrible. The French gunners set fire to the bridges over the river and many more Russians drowned in their efforts to get across and away from the French guns.

Napoleon won his battle because Lannes was able to hold the Russians for some six hours until the arrival of the main army. Napoleon took in the tactical situation at once and was able to make maximum use of both the terrain and his guns. He was able to mass his artillery in such large units at the appropriate spots that he produced a degree of firepower hitherto unknown in the history of warfare.

Friedland made Alexander sue for peace. He and Napoleon met for talks at Tilsit in 1807, and the impressionable and foolish young man now fell under the emperor's extraordinary charm. Tsar and emperor agreed to become joint masters of Europe. They would, if necessary, enter into an alliance against Turkey, should she refuse to make peace with Russia, and Russia would declare war on England should she refuse the tsar's offers of mediation.

Having defeated the Russians and overpowered Alexander with his personal charm, having convinced the Prussians that they could not defeat him in the field, while Austria still remembered her humiliation at Austerlitz, Napoleon was at the height of his power. His sphere of influence extended from the Pyrennees to the Pacific—in view of his alliance with Alexander—and he was in a position to impose his will upon virtually an entire continent.

It is quite proper to think of Napoleon's system of government as the imposition of a personal will. His civil service and his military commanders were supremely efficient at executing his orders. His generals were not however encouraged to think or act for themselves. The civil service was a little different in that Napoleon was so often absent from Paris, yet even here it has been suggested that he sought to administer France personally, down to the level of *préfet*. Certainly one prefect observed that the emperor exercised "the miracle of his real presence upon his servants however far they might be away from him." It is indeed true that never in modern times has a civil service been so highly motivated, prepared to work so hard, been so dedicated to processes of rapid and efficient government.

The energy with which his army and his administrators were imbued flowed from his own person. His correspondence amounts to thirty-two volumes; he must have dictated some 80,000 letters and orders in the course of his career. His handwriting, incidentally, was so bad that he was frequently unable to read it himself—a characteristic typical of the sort of rapid intellect which makes connections with lightning speed and will not wait upon the hand to catch up with the mind. The emperor would get up at 7 A.M. to read and dictate until nine, when he would receive his ministers. He always dressed simply, unlike many of his generals and marshals who were given to extraordinary magnificence in their choice of uniform. His tailor complained that he spent too little on clothes. Neither was he greatly interested in food or drink, nor indeed in sex although he had occasional liaisons and produced two illegitimate sons to make up for those which Joséphine failed to bear. The rest of

his day he would spend working on papers, or in conference, and would retire early, around
10 P.M., after putting in a twelve-hour working day.

When he had to, he could go without sleep almost indefinitely, although he would have to
make up for it in due course. Although it has been suggested that he had a peculiar metabolism
which enabled him to sustain extraordinary pressure for long periods, this was not the case.
Simply, Napoleon was driven by a concentrated passion, by a will, which had an utterly
exceptional intensity. All his enormous energies were focused, constantly, on his political
and military ambitions. He had no other interests, and his capacity for work came from his
vitality, his nerves, and his frugal way of life. Yet eventually even he was broken by it. As a
young man Napoleon had been an energetic, slim figure with an almost boyish beauty. Yet
by 1805 he had already begun to age prematurely, his health was deteriorating, he had twice
experienced crises which were remarkably close to epileptic seizures. He himself recognized
that the pace at which he ruled and fought could not be sustained for ever. Indeed in the later
years of his reign his health grew steadily worse. He became corpulent, aged, suffered from
skin trouble, bladder trouble, a bad stomach. He lost his energy and with it much of that
supreme clarity of vision which had earlier enabled him to see his chances and take them
unerringly. By the time of Waterloo he had slowed down so much that he appeared to
observers to be a parody of his early self.

As a ruler Napoleon believed that he could only succeed through absolute control over
his subjects; a control to be achieved through the "fear I inspire." He did not believe that
generosity made for an efficient principle of government; fear alone was infallible. He had a
poor view of humanity, had seen too many court his favor, crowned heads among them, to
have any but the most jaundiced view of those over whom he triumphed. He was, in one
sense, a very cold man, who never allowed personal feelings to override political considera-
tions. However, the feelings he entertained for Joséphine, the distress caused him by the
news of her infidelities, his mention of her as he died, all suggest a degree of emotional
commitment that is stronger than one might suspect at first sight. Equally, his second wife
and the son he had by her were to play strongly and tragically upon his affections at the end.
It would indeed to wrong to suppose that Napoleon was a totally cold fish. He loved to charm,
loved company and conversation. He fascinated almost everyone who met him—and yet this
fascination was not the vulgar magnetism of a Hitler: it came from charm and animation,
combined with a profound intelligence and great lucidity. He was capable of disarming
enemies with his frankness, of securing the loyalties of the meanest soldier in his army by
pinching his ear and talking to him intimately. There can be no doubt that he enjoyed the
power and the loyalty which such actions won him. For example, when writing from Poland
to the Chancellor of the Légion d'Honneur he said, "write to Corporal Bernaudet of the 13th
of the Line and tell him not to drink so much and behave better." He must have known,
with a deadly certainty, what an overpowering effect this would have upon the corporal in
question. One feels that ultimately he must have despised that corporal, and Tsar Alexander,
and countless others, for the ease with which his charm could win them over, just as Don
Juan despises the victims he cannot fail to seduce. Indeed, Napoleon was a kind of political
Don Juan, combining great coldness of soul, great intellect and a remarkable capacity to
have his way with others, a process which he found enjoyable at the time.

Yet he seldom openly abused the loyalties which he inspired. His marshals, generals, officers and men adored him. His presence on the battlefield was said to be worth 40,000 troops. Moreover he remained prepared to reward old friendships with high commands; too high sometimes. Equally he rewarded his family with a strangely vulgar generosity by placing them upon the thrones of Europe. Joseph was first king of Naples, then of Spain; Louis, king of Holland, was offered the Spanish throne, which he declined; Jérôme was king of Westphalia. His sister Camille married Murat, who succeeded Joseph on the throne of Naples. The appointments have a ring of wilful extravagance about them, a kind of comic-opera quality. However, it should be said that he never permitted his ruling brothers to rule. He expected absolute obedience from them, and when he did not get it he raged. Indeed here may lie the answer to the quality and nature of his choices. He would rather appoint obedient mediocrities, or members of his family, than persons of outstanding merit and perhaps questionable loyalty. He always remained a realist who never forgot how fragile his power base remained.

In 1806 Napoleon launched an economic war against England with the so-called Continental System, which was designed to deny her access to the export markets of Europe. At first it had very little effect because Napoleon had insufficient control over the coastline of Europe, while England was able to export a great deal to the United States. However, after the Treaty of Tilsit things began to change as Russia joined the system. Although it never brought England to its knees it did provide serious grounds for alarm, and it is arguable that had it not been for the Peninsular War and, later, the invasion of Russia, the system would eventually have brought Britain to the negotiating table. Yet paradoxically it was, in part at least, his desire to impose the system on the whole of Europe that made for Napoleon's most serious mistakes, first in Spain and then in Russia.

Spain was ruled by a decaying Bourbon monarchy: Charles IV, Maria Louisa and the favorite, Godoy. They were not an impressive trinity. They had maintained an alliance with France since 1804, largely because Godoy had his eye upon the throne of Portugal. At the end of 1806 Napoleon insisted that Spain join his Continental System, and in 1807 prepared an army for the invasion of Portugal, which was to be partitioned. The south would go to Godoy, and the north to the queen of Etruria who was to be removed from Tuscany to make room for Napoleon's sister Elisa. However, the king of Spain's son Ferdinand, fearing that Godoy would succeed his father, began to intrigue with Napoleon. The latter now made the first great mistake of his career. A rising at Aranjeuz had made Charles abdicate and Godoy resign. Napoleon now forced the Bourbons to go into exile and offered the throne of Spain to his brother Louis. He refused, and so he gave it to Joseph instead, and the Bonaparte family moved round once more. Napoleon did not realize that the Spanish people were fiercer, more patriotic, conservative and Catholic than any he had hitherto encountered. Anti-French movements sprang up all over the country, regular troops being supported by guerrillas. Napoleon had supposed there to be a large liberal faction which would receive him with open arms, and expected any unrest to be easily pacified. He was wrong on both counts. Moreover, Spanish terrain did not lend itself to the Napoleonic method of waging war. With his emphasis on maximum mobility, he never believed in large baggage trains or supply services, and required his armies to live off the country. It was a policy that had worked well enough in more fertile regions, but it was scarcely appropriate to Spain.

By 1808 two of Napoleon's generals had been defeated on the peninsula; Junot by the English at Vimiero, and Dupont, who was obliged to surrender to a Spanish army at Baylen. The French army was no longer invincible. Napoleon was told by his brother Joseph that his policies had proved disastrous, antagonizing the entire population, yet he declined to go back on them. A leader like Napoleon or, to a lesser degree, Hitler, who relies on his reading of a situation, acts on it, and has a long run of successes behind him, finds it almost impossible to admit to mistakes. Once he concedes that his intuition is fallible he can never trust it again, and the whole basis of his leadership, unshakable faith in self, is undermined for ever. Napoleon had committed himself to Spain and there could be no going back.

He was obliged to transfer the bulk of his army from Germany to Spain, having received promises of Russian neutrality from Alexander. He arrived in Madrid in December 1808, and attacked the English expeditionary force under Sir John Moore. However, Napoleon, having set up the campaign for Marshal Soult, returned to France early in the new year. Had he remained in Spain things might have gone differently. But Moore, who nearly lost his army at Corunna, was able to retreat and evacuate. Later in 1809 a new British force commanded by Sir Arthur Wellesley, the future Duke of Wellington, landed and obliged Soult to retreat. An English army was to remain on the peninsula despite efforts to dislodge it, and this presence, together with constant harrassment by Spanish irregulars, constituted a permanent threat from the southwest, and tied down large numbers of French troops. It gave the English a foothold in Europe, moreover. Perhaps the war could have been won had Napoleon assumed personal command, or even appointed a supreme commander. Instead he favored a divided command. The men were poorly paid, there was much corruption, frequent atrocities and a significant deterioration in morale. In due course Wellington would invade the southwest of France, and the last battle he fought there against Soult, at Toulouse on April 10, 1814, took place after Napoleon's abdication. Looking back from St. Helena he admitted that he had made a fatal error when he deposed the Bourbons. He described the "immorality of the proceedings" as having been "too great."

Patriotic resistance to Napoleon soon spread to other parts of Europe. One should recall that the concepts of patriotism and nationalism were not known in the civilized Europe of the eighteenth century. First encountered in Revolutionary France, there was now a general awakening of nationalistic consciousness throughout the continent. In the principalities of a divided Germany there began to grow the longing for a united nation independent of Napoleon, a feeling born in the defeat of Jena. Certain reforms instituted in the Prussian government were to lead to the formation of a popular militia, the emancipation of the serfs and changes in the structure of government. In Austria too a new spirit was abroad, and it seemed that Napoleon's Spanish setback provided an ideal opportunity to move against him once again.

Austria declared war on April 9, 1809, assuming that the relative weakness of French forces in Germany, and the need to flesh out the *grande armée* with new recruits, would give them the advantage. They were wrong. By dint of brilliant planning Napoleon rapidly concentrated his whole army in Bavaria. He fought a series of battles, Regensburg, Landshut and Eckmühl, which Napoleon always felt had been some of his finest. Yet they were inconclusive. The Austrians were able to withdraw, although it is true that they had suffered heavy losses. On May 12 Napoleon entered Vienna.

Next month, anxious to finish the Austrians before the Prussians intervened, Napoleon occupied the island of Lobau on the Danube. However, the Austrians attacked in force, at Aspern, and obliged Napoleon to concentrate his entire army on the island. They were short of provisions, ammunition and medical supplies. The action could be described as Napoleon's first defeat, leaving him in a situation dangerously close to that of the Russians at Friedland.

Yet cornered, Napoleon was at his most dangerous. He managed to turn the island into a strongpoint, with its bridge to the mainland protected by a flotilla of boats. At the same time he denuded his lines of communication in order to get all the reinforcements he could, and built up a massive concentration of troops. By July 4 he began to cross the Danube, and on the following day he met the Austrians at the village of Wagram. After a day of probing and testing Napoleon concluded that the Austrian center was weak. He concentrated his main forces, at the expense of his wings, ready to break through the following day. In the meantime Archduke Charles attacked the French left, an attack which Masséna managed to hold off. Napoleon then threw 30,000 men through the Austrian center. Yet the battle, in one sense, was not conclusive. The Austrian army was not annihilated and losses were heavy on both sides. A French victory it may have been, but it was certainly no Austerlitz. Although Austria was obliged to sue for peace, a peace which limited her territory and required her to pay a vast indemnity, Napoleon sensed that there was a different mood abroad. Wagram had been expensive. His troops had shown signs of panic, his losses had been severe. He had come to realize that he could not afford such victories indefinitely. He also sensed that Europe and the nature of the opposition were changing. It would seem that he was no longer prepared to consider battle as an infallible trump card.

Yet for the moment all seemed to favor Napoleon. The Austrians had recognized once again that they were not able to defeat the French single-handed. In the circumstances it seemed preferable to make an ally of their emperor. Moreover, Napoleon was increasingly anxious to consolidate his dynasty with an heir.

Joséphine had proved unable to bear him children. Since she had had a son and a daughter by her first marriage Napoleon had assumed the deficiency to be his own. However, the sons born to him by Eléonore Denuelle and Maria Walewska, Comte Léon and Comte Walewski as they were known, had set those doubts at rest. He had no wish to divorce Joséphine, but reasons of state came first. He had in fact been contemplating divorce since 1807, and finally decided to go through with it on December 16, 1809, when his marriage was finally annulled.

Napoleon had initially looked to Russia for a second wife. He had suggested to Alexander that he might marry his sister, Grand Duchess Catherine. Alexander had declined to commit himself, knowing how fiercely the suggestion would have been rejected by his own family. Meanwhile she had married the Duke of Oldenburg. Napoleon then made an offer of marriage to her younger sister, aged fifteen. The offer was rejected. Napoleon thereupon suggested to the Austrian ambassador that he marry the eldest daughter of his emperor, Marie-Louise, and was accepted immediately. The Corsican adventurer Bonaparte was marrying a member of one of the oldest dynasties in Europe.

The alliance established between Alexander and Napoleon at Tilsit had been under strain for some time. Although they had had an apparently cordial meeting at Erfurt the failure to achieve a marriage alliance was symptomatic of a certain deterioration. Alexander's adherence to the Continental System had not been popular at home, and there was a powerful element at court that considered Napoleon to be a force for evil tantamount to Antichrist. At the same time, although Napoleon had suggested a joint Russian-French expedition to India, there was a serious stumbling block, namely Constantinople. Russian foreign policy required control over Constantinople and the straits, a concession which Napoleon would never be prepared to grant since it would give Russia access to the Mediterranean. If agreement could not be reached on this point, possibility of a lasting alliance was out of the question.

Napoleon's commitment to an Austrian marriage made matters go from bad to worse. In December 1810 Alexander left the Continental System, and the following August Napoleon decided that war was inevitable. As he saw it defeat of Russia would bring the whole of Europe under his control and ensure the success of the Continental System, which would in turn bring England to heel and in due course make him master of the world.

By this stage in his career Napoleon no longer took advice. His ablest ministers, such as Talleyrand and Fouché, had resigned and he had surrounded himself with mediocrities and yes-men. Whether he was ever capable of being influenced by advice is an open question, but certainly the decisions he now made were entirely his own, and they were not taken in the light of discussion with anyone worth listening to. He seems to have been spurred by the vision of an Alexander the Great-like domination, as a contemporary observed: "What ideas. What dreams. It was halfway between Bedlam and the Pantheon."

His ambassador had warned him of the intransigent patriotism of the Russians, and of the rigor of their climate. He had moreover predicted that the Russians would retreat and draw their enemy into their country. Napoleon dismissed such warnings summarily. He based his assessments on the feeble character of Alexander, and although he was accurate enough in his view of the man, he made the mistake of confusing him with his people. True, he had routed the Russians at Austerlitz and Friedland, but just as he failed to appreciate the temper of the Spanish, so he could not understand that a Russian fighting abroad and a Russian defending his own soil were opponents of very different kinds.

He did not, however, underestimate the problems presented by such a campaign. He made complex preparations and recognized the project as "the most difficult enterprise I have so far attempted." He realized that he would need supply trains and elaborate lines of communication. It was to be a different kind of campaign in other respects too. Napoleon would invade with overwhelming numerical superiority; nearly half a million men opposed to Russian forces of some 200,000. Although this might appear to have given him the advantage it was in fact to count against Napoleon. He was always at his best fighting a mobile, fluid war. Now, with a huge army and massive baggage trains, he was denying himself that very mobility which brought out his genius.

In the build-up to the campaign Napoleon obtained the support of Austria and Prussia, who supplied him with second-line troops. However, he failed to secure the neutrality of England. Sweden, too, joined the Russians, and Turkey also signed a peace treaty with them. Alexander was thus free to deal with Napoleon alone, all threats to his flanks having been removed.

The *grande armée* crossed the Niemen in June 1812 and met with strictly limited opposition. Alexander was almost persuaded to stand and fight at a fortified camp at Drissa, withdrawing only just before the French arrived. The Russian command was divided between

Barclay de Tolly and Bagration, and, as they continued to withdraw, the French failed conspicuously in their efforts to trap them. Their advance continued with Napoleon perpetually expecting his enemy to stand and fight. He hoped for a battle at Vitebsk but the Russians withdrew overnight. Napoleon was now strongly urged by his marshals to end the campaign. Supplies were not getting through and the army was suffering severe losses from "natural wastage," i.e., desertion and disease, and losses that included some 20,000 horses. Napoleon agreed at first, announcing that they would stop where they were, but two days later he decided to continue his advance. He felt that the campaign must end with a major battle, and felt sure that the Russians would stand either at Smolensk or Moscow. Unless their army were to be defeated in the field he would have achieved nothing.

When he reached Smolensk on August 17 Napoleon was convinced that the Russians would make a stand and give him the battle he wanted. Yet again he failed to seal off their line of retreat and again they fell back. His effective army was now greatly reduced and chances of a decisive victory were fading fast. Yet, as with Spain, only on a larger and more critical scale, Napoleon would not go back on a plan of action to which he had committed himself. Instead he pressed on to Moscow. In the meantime, Alexander had appointed Kutuzov commander-in-chief of his army. He did not love the man, believing him to have been obliquely implicated in the assassination of his father and resenting him for the defeat which his own rashness had brought about at Austerlitz. However, sheer weight of public opinion obliged the tsar to put his most able commander at the head of his armies. Kutuzov had the greatest respect for Napoleon, and the respect was mutual. The "Fox of the North," as Napoleon dubbed him, was to be the enemy that he feared most.

Kutuzov never believed that the task of an army was to gain or hold terrain. Territory for him was a basis for maneuvering to destroy the enemy, and had no value in itself. He had been prepared to let Napoleon have Vienna once before; now he was ready to fall back beyond Moscow. However, the weight of opinion insisting that Russia's ancient capital be defended proved too much for him and he felt obliged to take up a defensive position at the village of Borodino.

The ensuing battle was one of the bloodiest ever fought. The Russians were in a well-defended position with fortified redoubts which the French attacked repeatedly. They were taken and retaken several times in bitter hand-to-hand fighting. The battle was no elegant display of tactics, with little to delight the armchair strategist. Indeed both Kutuzov and Napoleon played strangely ineffective roles, well away from the front line. Certainly in the Russians' case this made, at times, for less than perfect coordination. Borodino was a soldiers' not a generals' battle, in which two armies fought to their limit. The decisive moment that Napoleon felt should come in every battle was never found here. Instead there was the awesome spectacle of two armies holding on to the limits of endurance and beyond. The French could scarcely advance another step, and kept coming; the Russians could not hold out another moment, but stayed their ground. The casualties were dreadful; the French lost 35,000 and the Russians 50,000. Had Napoleon committed his Imperial Guard, the cream of his armies, he would certainly have carried the day, but only at the risk of having no army left at the end of it. He later described the affair as "the most terrible of all my battles . . . The French showed themselves worthy of victory, and the Russians worthy of being invincible."

Kutuzov decided to withdraw and abandon Moscow, retreating through the city. Napoleon entered expecting to be greeted by a deputation. Instead he found the city abandoned. Fires were started, probably by order of the governor, Rostopchin, and it was some days before they could be brought under control.

Napoleon took up residence in the Kremlin and waited for Alexander to negotiate. He sent emissaries, via Kutuzov, but these were fobbed off and their offers subsequently rejected. In the meantime Kutuzov was rebuilding his army which he then secretly redeployed to the southwest of Moscow in order to deny Napoleon the fertile territories that lay there when he should eventually come out. French intelligence was lamentably inadequate and the emperor had no idea of these movements until it was too late.

Napoleon ignored repeated warnings about the Russian winter, and, indeed, autumn that year was singularly bright and mild. One of the greatest omissions was the failure to shoe horses for ice and snow. As a result practically the whole of the French cavalry would vanish in the ensuing retreat, a loss that could never be made up.

On October 19, finally persuaded that there would be no negotiations, Napoleon came out of Moscow. He wanted to take the southern, Kaluga road, but found Kutuzov barring it in force. A hard day's fighting convinced him that he would not be able to break through. He retreated and accepted that he would have to return the way he had come—even though this would mean withdrawing over territory already pillaged for food and fodder. It is arguable that had Kutuzov attacked, rather than allowing the French to escape, he might have annihilated them, but throughout this campaign the Fox of the North would prove singularly reluctant to press home military advantage.

Napoleon continued to retreat in conditions of increasing hardship as frosts and then snow came. His army was harrassed by Cossacks and irregulars; anyone leaving his unit for a moment was all too likely to be cut down. They were terribly short of stores, the horses were dying and discipline fading fast. Napoleon, using his Guard, broke through one attempt at encirclement at Krasnoy, but was obliged to abandon his rearguard, commanded by Ney. Rather than surrender they fought their way through, rejoining the main body with 800 men left of the original 8,000.

The next obstacle was the River Beryezina. It was imperative that the French should cross before two Russian armies joined forces to face them. The Russian advance guard was driven back from the river, but only after they had destroyed the bridges over it. A certain hesitancy on the part of the Russian commander Chichagov gave the French time to build new ones. The crossing began on November 26 at 4 P.M. as the Russians began to close in. Crossing continued all night under heavy fire, and went on the following day. A determined attack by the Russians at 8 A.M. was repelled by the rearguard after bitter fighting. By 1 P.M. the army was safely across. It is said that of the 26,000 men engaged in the fight at the river only 900 were fit for duty the next day. By the time the *grande armée* had fallen back to Vilna it was no more than a starving rabble. Napoleon had written to his foreign minister there, telling him that on no account must foreign agents see the troops arrive: "The army is not a good sight today."

Bonaparte abandoned his army on December 6. He had received news of a conspiracy in Paris founded on rumors of his death. He left Murat in command, and returned to France almost alone. Of the original 450,000 men less than one in ten had survived.

Napoleon was under some pressure to make peace, even if this meant that France would have to withdraw to her "natural" frontier of the Rhine, the point of Napoleon's departure in 1799. In the meantime the neutrality negotiated with Prussia and Austria had disintegrated. King Frederick William of Prussia signed a treaty with the Russians on February 28, 1813, while the Austrians preferred to wait. Metternich, Austria's foreign minister, urged Napoleon to sue for peace. It is hard to say whether or not he was sincere, but there is reason to suppose that he would have accepted Napoleon, married to a Habsburg, on the throne of France. However, Napoleon was not prepared to sacrifice his gains. He felt that he could only maintain control over France as long as he had the prestige and authority conferred upon him by his empire. He could not afford a setback, could not be seen to lose, for the day he lost his strength he would lose his authority. It is impossible to say whether his assessment was correct, and certainly it sounds like the rationalization of his compulsive need to continue the fight. In the meantime he did not take Metternich's offer seriously, nor did he think that the Austrians posed any kind of threat, for he could not accept that his father-in-law would wage war against him.

The Prussians and the Russians, against the advice of the dying Kutuzov, continued to press the French armies. Napoleon fought them twice at Lützen and Bautzen, battles which were far from decisive but quite enough to check their advance and leave them depressed. He subsequently agreed to an armistice and a peace conference. Metternich now again pressed Napoleon to settle for the Rhine frontiers, but the terms were unacceptable to him. Napoleon's attitude only succeeded in convincing Metternich that he would never accept peace of any kind, and that negotiation with him was not possible. The talks came to nothing, and in the meantime Napoleon proceeded to build up his German army. He had some 470,000 men against the Allies, who could field about half a million.

The campaign of 1813 was well short of Napoleon's best form. The allies were grouped in three separate armies, north, center and west, and one might have expected Napoleon to engage in rapid and decisive action to prevent them from joining. It may be that it was the lack of efficient cavalry, the result of the Russian campaign, that impeded him and reduced his mobility. Whatever the reason, his movements were strangely hesitant. He first advanced on the Prussians and Berlin, but, learning that another army was attacking Dresden, he brought his men back in an extraordinary forced march, covering ninety miles in seventy-two hours, to enter Dresden in force shortly before the allied attack. The ensuing battle was to be the last great victory of the *grande armée*, and it failed to destroy the Allies. Dresden was followed by a series of abortive attempts to catch the Prussians, attempts which wore Napoleon's army down. For a month or so he was utterly indecisive in command, uncertain of his objectives and unable to act positively, while his army was steadily reduced by sickness and desertion. He planned to strike at the three allied armies separately but failed to seize his opportunities. He could have caught one of them before the others joined it, but he missed his chance. On October 17 the three armies were united: Napoleon was outnumbered two to one. At the Battle of Leipzig the French, though defeated, withdrew in good order, but they left some 60,000 men, including 20,000 prisoners, behind them. They found their line of retreat blocked at Hanau by a Bavarian army of 50,000 with over a hundred cannon, but after some outstanding artillery maneuvers they launched a frontal assault and practically destroyed the lot. Nevertheless, by the time that Napoleon crossed the Rhine his army was reduced to 60,000 men—as many as he had lost at Leipzig.

There were further attempts to negotiate a peace. France herself was exhausted, and yet Napoleon's methods of conscription allowed him to raise a new army which, in practical terms, amounted to 120,000 men. The ensuing campaign of 1814 was a sad affair. Despite the physical and financial exhaustion of his country Napoleon still hoped to win. He called on his generals to "repeat the campaign of Italy" when his impoverished army had won battle after battle. Indeed it is ironic that, for many military historians, the 1814 campaign was the most brilliant that Napoleon ever fought, but it was a wasted brilliance. His plan was based on the assumption that Paris would hold out as an armed fortress, enabling him to use his army to attack the enemy's lines of communication and take them in the rear. He was vastly outnumbered, yet paradoxically the disproportion was almost an advantage, for it permitted him to make use of the mobility that had always been his strongest suit as a commander.

He learned that the allied armies had separated as they advanced into France. The Austrians under Schwarzenberg were advancing along the Seine, Blücher's Prussians along the Marne. This gave him his chance. He caught Blücher at Champaubert, and then at Montmirail, hurting him badly. Three days later he routed him at Vauchamps, inflicting casualties of 10,000. Then four days after that he defeated Schwarzenberg at Montereau. Schwarzenberg wanted an armistice, but Castlereagh, the English foreign secretary, made the Allies pledge themselves not to negotiate a separate peace with Napoleon. In the meantime Wellington was advancing into southwestern France.

Napoleon now suffered a serious setback when he lost 6,000 men at Craonne. The disparity in numbers was growing too great for him to hope to be able to fight for much longer. His brother Joseph, who was governor of Paris, and his wife Marie-Louise were both urging him to make peace. He still had a chance however—to retreat east into Lorraine, collect reinforcements and take the Allies in the rear. The plan was based on the assumption that Paris would hold out. Unfortunately the Allies intercepted a letter of his to Marie-Louise outlining the plan, and this determined Tsar Alexander to insist that the advance on Paris be continued. The city fell on March 30, 1814, after the battle of Montmartre. There was an element of betrayal about its capitulation. Joseph had been less than positive in his governorship and Talleyrand, never one to linger on a sinking ship, had disobeyed an order of Napoleon's to remove the government to Rambouillet. Instead he allowed the empress to depart and stayed behind to negotiate with the Allies. Treason, he once observed was "a matter of dates." Napoleon tried to abdicate in favor of his son the king of Rome, with a regency, hoping that his army would support the plan. He was bluntly informed that they would not, and it was made clear to the emperor that his only option was an unconditional abdication, which he signed on April 6, 1814.

The Treaty of Fontainbleau recognized that Napoleon was still entitled to call himself Emperor. Unfortunately his empire was limited to the few square miles of the island of Elba. He was to reign there with a revenue of two million francs payable by the French government. The empress was granted the duchy of Parma, where she would be succeeded by her son. It is worth remarking that Napoleon had attained the age of forty-five.

He was desperately anxious that his wife and son should join him, terrified that they would come entirely under the influence of the Austrians. When it became clear that this would indeed be the case he reached an extreme of despair. He tried to kill himself by taking poison, but the draft had lost its potency and he recovered after an uncomfortable night. The Austrians at no time had any intention of permitting Marie-Louise and the king of Rome to remain with Napoleon. They saw it as imperative that the boy be brought up an Austrian, that Napoleon be isolated and Marie-Louise protected from him. She initially took the enforced separation hard. There is reason to suppose that she and Napoleon felt more for one another than the affections one might associate with an imperial marriage of convenience. There can be no doubt that Napoleon adored his son. The conclusion of his relationship with his wife is unlovely. Metternich imposed upon her as an aide-de-camp a certain General Neipperg, who had his instructions and carried them out. By the time that Napoleon died Neipperg had given her two children. When she became Duchess of Parma she married him, and on his death married her prime minister.

Napoleon ruled Elba with efficiency and application. There was nothing lax about the etiquette of his court. Meanwhile, the Bourbon dynasty, in the shape of Louis XVIII, had been restored in Paris, and Paris had not received it warmly. The Bourbons did not treat their conquered enemy generously, declining to pay him his revenue of two million francs. Napoleon grew increasingly restless. He was especially enraged by talk of his cowardice, his fear of death, and driven, moreover, by the despair of a forty-five-year-old adventurer without prospects, and with no adventures left.

On March 1, 1815, he landed at Antibes with about a thousand men. As he advanced north he was greeted with enthusiasm and acclaim. At Grenoble he found an infantry regiment standing across the road, and advanced to face them alone, inviting them to: "Kill your emperor if you wish." Instead the regiment streamed across to join him and was shortly followed by the entire garrison. Unit after unit deserted the Bourbons for their old commander, and by March 20 he was carried up the steps of the Tuileries by an exultant crowd; the culmination of a progress through France which he would describe as the happiest period of his life.

Napoleon had considerable military resources on which he could now draw, including many returned prisoners of war. The allied armies were dispersed along the Belgian frontier, and his task, as always, was to smash them one by one before they could join up. He was able to place 120,000 men on the frontier before they even knew that he was on the move. When he made contact at Ligny on June 16 he planned to use his left, commanded by Ney, to attack the Prussians and drive them away from Wellington. He should have succeeded, but poor staff work prevented the reserve from being committed and the Prussians got away, with a severe mauling, from what should have been a rout. Yet had Napoleon acted decisively the next day the Prussians might still have been destroyed, but, as with the Leipzig campaign, his clarity of vision seems to have failed him. He hesitated too long and allowed the Allies to gain the initiative. In due course the Prussians, under Blücher, would be able to join Wellington at Waterloo, while Grouchy, who had been sent in pursuit of them, was to arrive too late. Bad generals, bad orders, bad liaison may be said to have cost Napoleon the battle.

Waterloo was not one of his finest pieces of strategy. He had never faced Wellington before and underestimated the quality of his generalship and the quality of his men, particularly the firepower of the English infantry. He did not take personal command of the battle, leaving it to Ney, and it has been suggested that a seriously upset stomach kept him away from the battlefield for much too long. Whatever the reason, French tactics have been described as disastrous. They began with massive infantry attacks in column, which were dreadfully expensive and ineffectual. This was followed by a series of cavalry charges which failed to break the English squares. When both infantry and cavalry failed the Imperial Guard were committed, early in the evening, and when their attack was repelled the French broke and ran. It has been suggested that Napoleon's mistake was to permit infantry and cavalry to attack separately—had he committed them together the result would have been very different. It is the kind of observation much beloved by armchair strategists, and one cannot help feeling that Napoleon must have considered this obvious possibility and rejected it for good reason. Even as it was Wellington considered that he had come within a whisker of defeat so that perhaps the tactics were not, after all, entirely disastrous.

Napoleon returned to Paris in a torpor, to find that he had lost all popular support. He decided to abdicate again, in favor of the king of Rome, and planned to sail to America. However, he left his departure so late that the harbor of Rochefort was blockaded by the English, and Napoleon resolved to throw himself upon the mercy of his enemy. He wrote to the Prince Regent that he was coming "like Themistocles to appeal to the hospitality of the British people." He then embarked for England on the *Bellerophon*. He was treated with the utmost respect on board and when they reached England sightseers flocked round the ship, and they too were very far from hostile.

The English government was less well disposed towards him, indeed there was a strong feeling that he should be handed over to the French for execution. At all events there could be no question of his remaining in England, as he had hoped. Instead General Buonaparte, as he was henceforward to be known, was dispatched to the island of St. Helena and permitted a retinue of three officers and twelve servants.

The voyage took three months and Napoleon endured its discomforts cheerfully. He did not take to the island itself. His accommodation there was well short of Imperial, especially at first. However, St. Helena had compensations, strange ones. Napoleon made close friends with the two young daughters of William Balcombe, an agent of the East India Company. He would engage them in conversations such as:

"Who burnt Moscow?"

"I do not know, sir."

"Yes, yes, it was I who burnt it."

"I believe, sir, that the Russians burnt it to get rid of the French."

Whereupon the portly ex-emperor would collapse with laughter. The two girls teased him mercilessly, and he replied in kind. On one occasion they got hold of his ceremonial sword and forced him into a corner with it. He retaliated by cheating outrageously at whist. Once, when the girls got too boisterous, their mother locked them away in the cellar, and Napoleon fed them sweets through the bars. His aides were horrified at the lack of decorum displayed by the English teenagers, and reproached Napoleon for permitting it. He greeted their pompous remonstrations with the strangely sad and moving observation that he felt himself to be "at a masked ball."

In the early days of his exile he was allowed to ride about the island freely, and to receive visitors. He seems to have been cheerfully resigned, and certainly not lacking in humor. Yet with the arrival of the new governor of the island, Hudson Lowe, probably the most hated

English name in French history, things changed. Lowe was a stiff-necked fool, terrified that Napoleon would escape, seeing nothing but espionage and conspiracy about him. He ordered Napoleon to reduce his household, insisted on reading all incoming and outgoing mail, and forbade Napoleon to ride unsupervised. All visitors had to be provided with passes. It is understandable that the man who had ruled over most of Europe took against such restrictions. A terrible series of clashes ensued, and Napoleon, in his final interview, described the governor as a clerk and a hangman. In his will, too, he talks of the English oligarchy's "hired assassin" (pages 36–7). He won a few concessions, being released from the obligation to report to an orderly officer twice a day, but only when he threatened to shoot anyone entering his apartments. However, it is true to say that Lowe remained a source of intense aggravation to Napoleon. He was also responsible for the deterioration in the emperor's health, in that he was reluctant to continue his rides under the conditions that Lowe had laid down for them.

St. Helena was not a healthy place; it was well known for its effects upon the liver and it seems likely that Napoleon contracted hepatitis, although some people, mostly French, have alleged that the English fed him arsenic. Official English policy preferred to let it be believed that he was shamming; two naval doctors who suggested the contrary were dismissed from the service. His illness was considered to be "diplomatic." Throughout this period Napoleon was subject to fainting fits, vomiting and acute loss of appetite. On April 23, 1821, an English doctor recognized that he was unwell and would take a long time to recover, but did not feel that there was any danger. The next day he started to throw up something which ressembled "coffee grounds." On May 2 he received extreme unction and at 2 A.M. on May 5 he uttered his last words, words strangely moving and revealing: *"France, armée, tête d'armée, Joséphine."* That he should think of his country, his army, his command, one may understand, but that his last word of all should recall his faithless ex-wife gives his feelings for her a strange resonance, an enduring consistency which one would not otherwise have suspected of the emperor. Late in the afternoon on May 5 his doctor Antommarchi declared him dead.

Napoleon's military achievements need no comment. For twenty years he had carried France with him on his adventures and imposed himself upon the four corners of Europe. He had shaped a country in which anyone who had talent could feel that there were no limits to where his ambition might take him. He breathed fire and energy into an entire nation, and, for many who had served him, France after his departure was dead, stultified, claustrophobic. The country which had once been ablaze with uniforms, its bells ringing out one victory peal after another, was to become dominated by the sober livery of the banker's black frock-coat and the priest's *soutane.*

Yet Napoleon did more than infuse his nation with that sense of *gloire* which has been their inspiration ever since and, sometimes, their undoing. He also laid the foundations of a modern state. He restored centralization and set up an administrative system which has survived largely unaltered to the present day. He was responsible for setting up the *Code Civil,* the Council of State, the *Banque de France,* the modern universities. Indeed he gave France that centralized, planned and paternalistic system of government which she enjoys to this day. *Gloire* and centralization, these are his most important legacies. They have lasted much longer than his military achievements, and while it is arguable that they are a mixed blessing, it remains true that no individual in modern times has left such a lasting mark upon his country. The shrewdest of his contemporaries, Metternich and Talleyrand, took similar views of him. For Metternich he had: "but one passion, power, he never lost either his time or his means in objects which might have diverted him from this aim. Master of himself, he soon became master of events. In whatever time he had appeared he would have played a dominant part." For Talleyrand he was: "certainly a great, an extraordinary man, almost as extraordinary in his qualities as in his career . . . The most extraordinary man I ever saw, and I believe the most extraordinary man that has lived in our age or for many ages."

The will itself is a strange document. On the whole Napoleon's writings in exile ramble and lack incisiveness, but the will is different. It clearly betrays a political intent. It is almost as if Napoleon could foresee that France would be dominated by the "Napoleonic Legend." The sentimentalized view of the *petit caporal* pinching his soldiers' ears, leading them from victory to victory in his crusade against the reactionary crowned heads of Europe in an attempt to "liberate nations from their yoke," would play a vital part in the anti-Bourbon opposition of the years to come. It would still prove powerful enough to bring his nephew Louis Napoleon to power by *coup d'état* in 1851. The will feeds the legend well. It shows a Napoleon devoted to his beloved country. It expresses his opinion of the English. It reveals his certainly genuine concern and love for his son, and the fears, all too well founded, that he would be brought up an Austrian. It expresses his wish to be buried on the banks of the Seine—a wish which would be realized with much pomp and reverence in 1840. It assures the world of his devotion to the people of France.

Yet at the same time the will has a peculiarly unsettling strain to it. There is something extraordinary about the detail into which he enters with his clothes lists. He seems genuinely to have been able, *in extremis*, to enumerate precisely how many pairs of silk hose, how many pairs of gloves, were with him on his island. The quantities matter to him. When this is combined with the millions of francs he gives away, making legacies to persons whom he urges to make the appropriate marriages, the effect is uncanny. No less so is the brazen way in which he disposes of objects to which he has no title: "Frederick II's alarm clock, which I removed from Potsdam." His claims to the Italian civil list are equally questionable. The blend of grandiose bequest with detailed knowledge of the state of his personal linen is bizarre, the concentrated sense of detail uncanny. There is more here than a wish to perpetuate his legend, remind his son that he is a Bonaparte and reward his faithful servants.

Napoleon's possessions, whether real or imaginary, still appear real enough to him, and just as he would make the most careful dispositions before a battle, so now the emperor-adventurer avails himself of a very last opportunity to deploy and commit his possessions, doing everything to ensure that all goes according to plan. That not all the possessions are actually his is beside the point. In a manner which recalls Hitler in his bunker, throwing in division after division which have long since ceased to exist, Napoleon uses the opportunity afforded him by the drafting of a will to make one final battle plan, and, for the very last time and if only on paper, to exercise his power.

ALEX de JONGE

Commentary I

THE STORY OF Napoleon's will is involved and often confusing. The course of its drafting reflects the mind of an exile, sick, daily seeking to increase the number of legatees; endeavoring to omit no one who had served him; endeavoring to reward those remaining faithful to him to the last, favoring first one and then another according to his mood; attempting to make use of everything which, viewed from afar, still seemed to him to be his personal property, endeavoring above all to avoid the restrictions which the British government might impose upon the execution of his last wishes.

The checkered history of this document recalls the story of another French sovereign's will, that of Louis XIV, which was concealed within the wall of a tower of the *Palais de Justice* and disappeared altogether for over two hundred years, before being presented to the National Archives by Mme. Lucien Graux in memory of her husband, who died deported and who had been able to acquire the document for his famous collection of autographs.

The original of the emperor's will as preserved today in the National Archives consists of the following documents:

1. The will as such (paginated 1–14 in 1853), entirely in the emperor's own hand, signed, sealed and dated Longwood, April 15, 1821. It includes three inventories (a, A and B) listing certain objects, and signed by Napoleon. Lists b (silverware), and c (china), were drawn up on the same day but no longer feature in the will; they are known by copies.

2. The first codicil (paginated 15–18 in 1853), in the emperor's hand, signed, sealed and dated April 16. Together with the following document it contains the only part of the will that was to be communicated to the English: the return of the ashes to France (which picks up article 2 of the will) and the division of the emperor's property on St. Helena between Grand-Marshal Bertrand and Marchand, in order to prevent the property from being impounded. Lists of "boxes," snuff boxes, numbered I, II and III, dictated the same day, were originally attached to this document.

3. The second codicil (paginated 1–2), in the emperor's hand, signed sealed and dated April 16. This document completes the preceding one, stipulating that the will is to be opened in Europe, and naming Montholon, Bertrand and Marchand as its executors.

4. The third codicil (paginated 29–32 in 1853), written on April 21, 22 or 23, signed and dated the 24th, in the emperor's hand. It disposes of the crown jewels and the emperor's Elban revenues.

5. The fourth codicil (paginated 33–36 in 1853), written by the emperor on April 21, 22 or 23, signed and dated the 24th. It consists of legacies to people he knew at the start of his career, provides for legal expenses and nominates a treasurer. This document has lost its original envelope.

6. The codicil disposing of monies in the hands of Marie-Louise (paginated 37–40 in 1853), written between April 21 and 24 by the emperor, signed and dated the 24th.

7. The codicil (the sixth) distributing the proceeds of the Italian civil list currently held by Eugène de Beauharnais (paginated 19–28 in 1853, pages 20 and 27 being omitted by mistake). Written between the 21st and 24th by the emperor, signed and dated April 24.

8. Instructions to the executors (paginated 1–2), dictated to Marchand between the 22nd and the 25th, signed by Napoleon and dated April 26 by Marchand.

9. Letter to Laffitte, the emperor's banker, drafted to instructions by Montholon, recopied by Marchand and signed the same day by Napoleon, predating it April 25.

10. Letter to Baron de la Bouillerie, treasurer of the emperor's private estate, drafted to instructions by Montholon, recopied by Marchand on the 29th, signed that day by Napoleon, predated April 28.

To these texts in the National Archives three other documents must be added:

11. The seventh codicil. Its existence is confirmed by all the witnesses, and moreover codicils 5 and 6 refer to this "legacy of conscience." The text is known through copies (in particular those of the Murat papers in the National Archives). Composed between the 23rd and the 25th by the emperor, signed and dated the 25th, it consisted of legacies of conscience, including one to Count Léon, the emperor's son. For this reason it was declared that it would never be printed and would remain secret; not even the treasurer would know of it, it was to be destroyed as soon as it was executed; it would not be made available to inspection since it concerned matters of conscience. The codicil went the way of the will. It was known still to exist in England on August 5, 1825.

12. The eighth codicil. Its existence has been vouched for by Frédéric Masson. It was drawn up by the emperor on the 29th and antedated the 27th, but the sick man could only write for four paragraphs. Articles 5–7 and the last three words of article 2 were written by Montholon, who refrained from having the emperor sign the document, kept it with him and took it to England. It was attested in 1822 and 1823. The document was in London on June 17, 1938, at which time Mr. Hobson, the director of Sotheby's, sent a photograph of it to the National Archives in France. The text (already published by Jean Savant in 1951) reads as follows:

Thursday April 27, 1821
Sick in body but of sound mind, I have written the eighth codicil to my will in my own hand:

1. I name Montholon, Bertrand and Marchand my executors and Las Cases or his son my treasurer;

2. I request my much loved Marie-Louise to take into her service my surgeon Antommarchi, to whom I bequeath an annuity of 6,000 francs a year to be paid by her;

3. Similarly to take Vignali as almoner and to place him as such in the service of my son;

4. I leave my residence at Ajaccio, together with all my possessions, land, vineyards, gardens, furniture and livestock to my mother;

5. I bequeath all I own on Elba, house, furniture, vineyards, land, livestock to my dearest, most honored sister Princess Pauline;

6. I bequeath to Countess Bertrand and Countess Montholon half of my set of Sèvres porcelain—the other half is to go to my son.

7. I bequeath all my share in the estate jointly held with Cardinal Fesch in Corsica to the said cardinal.

13. An informal legacy to the Duke of Reichstadt, dictated rapidly to Marchand on the back of a playing card on the evening of April 29.

For fear that the British might confiscate his will Napoleon had made a second copy, partly in his own hand, of all his last wishes, dating it April 15 and sealing it with his seal. The copy was placed in the hands of his almoner Abbé Vignali, in the secrecy of the confessional, with instructions to convey it to Madame Mère, or Cardinal Fesch, failing that to one of the emperor's brothers, in order that it should be transmitted to his son when he reached the age of sixteen. This document, which has an introductory note by Bertrand, now rests in the archives of His Imperial Highness Prince Napoleon, and featured in the exhibition "Souvenirs of the Imperial Family," at the Chateau of Bois-Préau (Malmaison), in 1968, catalog no. 75.

It is now necessary to pinpoint the chronology of events which make up the history of these documents using Marchand's *Mémoires* (ed. Bourguignon and Lachouque, 1952), Bertrand's *Cahiers de Sainte-Hélène* (ed. Fleuriot de Langle, 1949), Montholon's *Récits de captivité* (1847), and M. Jean Savant's thorough study in the *Cahiers de l'Académie Napoléon*, September 1951.

As soon as he crossed on the *Bellerophon*, and later in August 1819, Napoleon had drawn up a first will and placed it in the hands of Bertrand. The emperor took it back on December 12, 1820, and Marchand returned it to Bertrand on April 9 or 10, 1821. Wishing to make certain alterations Napoleon closeted himself with Montholon on April 13 and dictated the draft of a second will; he transcribed it himself on April 15. The next day, in codicils 1 and 2, he assembled all the clauses that were to be shown to the British authorities, and nominated his executors: Montholon, Bertrand and Marchand. " 'My son,' he said to Montholon on the 14th, 'I feel it is time I finished.' Seated upon his bed, the emperor held a piece of cardboard in one hand and wrote with the other, unsupported; Count de Montholon held an ink-well." (Merchand's *Mémoires*.) On the 18th he had Montholon, Bertrand, Marchand and Vignali seal the three envelopes with red ribbon. They signed and sealed without seeing the contents. All papers were passed to Marchand. It was only then that the emperor realized that he had left contradictory instructions. The next day he sent Marchand to recover the first will from Bertrand, and it was burnt in his presence. Between the 21st and 25th he completed his list of legacies, drawing up instructions for his executors and composing five new codicils, one of which, the seventh, the "legacy of conscience," was to remain secret.

The documents were signed on the 24th, 25th, 26th, but on April 22 he said to Bertrand: "I have drawn up three wills. The first is only to be opened in Paris. You must say that it was brought by Buonavita [Abbé Buonavita, Madame Mère's chaplain, who came to St. Helena with Abbé Vignali in September 1819 and left on March 17, 1821] to Europe to prevent the English from finding it. The second is a codicil to be opened here and showed to the English, in which I dispose of all I have here in order to avoid them taking possession of it. The third is for the empress."

On April 27 at 9.30 P.M. the emperor had the same four witnesses seal the six new envelopes with green ribbon. Once again everything except the previously mentioned copy of the whole will was passed to Marchand. Two days later, much weakened, Napoleon decided to make further provisions to express his gratitude to Dr. Antommarchi; he predated it April 27 to include it in his will: this is the eighth codicil. But he stopped, exhausted, at the fourth paragraph and Montholon added the three clauses that follow, which include bequests to Countess Bertrand and Countess Montholon, without trying to get the emperor to sign them, although he had the strength to sign letters to Laffitte and La Bouillerie on that same day; Montholon revealed the contents to Bertrand but kept the document. The same day the emperor, whose mind was beginning to go, dictated the beginnings of a draft legacy to his son.

The emperor passed away at 5.45 P.M. on May 5, 1821. That evening Marchand passed to Montholon all the documents with which he had been entrusted. Montholon made a formal inventory in front of Marchand, Bertrand and Abbé Vignali, alluding to the eighth codicil. The second codicil was opened. The English governor, Hudson Lowe, who came to Longwood on the 6th, the day of the autopsy, returned on the 12th. The first codicil was opened in his presence; he also took note of the second. Two days later the three executors undertook, with his permission, the division of the emperor's effects in accordance with the second codicil.

Montholon, Bertrand, Marchand and Vignali set off for France on May 27 or 30. On board the *Camel*, in European waters, and, in accordance with the emperor's wishes, on the latitude of Paris, they gathered round Montholon and opened all the sealed envelopes—on July 25. Montholon did not show them the eighth codicil but appraised them of its contents. They disembarked at Calais on October 19, and Montholon hastened to Paris with his precious document, to have its instructions carried out. After having copies taken by the Seine Tribunal, and having had the letter to Laffitte duly notarized, he found himself involved in a protracted struggle with the emperor's banker in order to secure the release of the funds. On the advice of Cambacérès, and in order to secure a foreign guarantee of the documents, he crossed the Channel and lodged everything except for the eighth codicil with the clerk of the Court of Canterbury in London, the territory of St. Helena being within its competence. He entrusted the papers to Stephen Lushington, the deputy clerk. The court action against Laffitte, and the compromise of January 8, 1826, which greatly reduced the bequests which could be honored by the emperor's estate are well known. After the partial execution of the will matters were allowed to stand. Louis-Philippe then decreed the return of the ashes, which took place on December 15, 1840.

When he became emperor Napoleon III wished to establish the continuity of the imperial dynasty, and as a point of honor discharged all bequests made by his uncle. To do so he had to recover possession of the will, and Count Alexander Colonna Walewski, natural son of

Napoleon I and ambassador of Napoleon III, requested Queen Victoria for its return. The Court of Doctors' Commons, when consulted, agreed to pass the will, codicils 1, 2, 3, 4, 5, 6, and the two letters to Count Clarendon, First Secretary of State to Her Most Britannic Majesty, who presented them to Walewski on March 16, 1853. The documents were brought back to Paris and placed in the hands of Debelleyme, President of the Seine Tribunal, who numbered the pages and signed them on March 26. That same day they were stamped and formally deposited with the emperor's notary Casimir Noël; two missing documents were added in June or July: the second codicil and the instructions. No one knows what became of the seventh codicil. Napoleon III, by means of a commission established by a decree of August 5, 1854, and the credit of four million francs granted it, proceeded to fulfill all the will's instructions. By 1859 the affair was complete and the will became a historical document. In a letter of April 28, 1860, the emperor confided it to Count de Laborde, Director-General of the Imperial Archives, to be placed in the iron chest which held all the family documents of the ruling houses of France. It is still there.

JEAN-PIERRE BABELON
Curator of the Museum of French History

Commentary II

THE LAST DOCUMENT to have marked the noble destiny of Napoleon I was the will which he drew up entirely in his own hand when sick and at death's door, exhausted by suffering.

In itself that is remarkable enough. Over the years autographed letters from the emperor had grown increasingly scarce, and, signatures and marginal notes apart, it would take a matter of vital importance to persuade him to take pen in hand. But in the course of his last days, upon that lonely isle of misery which St. Helena was for him, and when the will of the Allies had removed him from the world, he desired to leave posterity one last, solemn document.

Early in April 1821 the emperor, with his usual clairvoyance, realized that his end was near and that the time had come to make his last dispositions. On April 11 he revealed his plan to Montholon, who had become his confidant since the departure of Las Cases and Gourgaud. The next day he began to dictate the basic outline of his will. He corrected the first draft on the 14th and work continued the following day, giving him some relief from his dreadful suffering.

He grew steadily worse and the English doctor Arnott and his team became alarmed at his symptoms. During the evening of April 27 Napoleon tried to get up to read his will in front of his executors, and to establish formally the circumstances of its composition.

It was the beginning of the end, but the next day he still had strength enough to give final instructions to his physician Antommarchi, who was to cut out his heart and take it to the Empress Marie-Louise. We all know how little store the Duchess of Parma set by that pious gift.

A first will, drawn up earlier and placed in the hands of Count Bertrand, had been burnt by order of Napoleon, to be superseded by a second one, and it was during these last days of lucidity that he had the new text copied, signing the copy at the foot of each section.

It is the original will which, together with its codicils and attached inventories, is now preserved in the National Archives, and features as the key document of the Empire in the Museum of French History.

This moving document shows that in his sorry plight the emperor had retained all his spirit and a flawless memory.

About to die in a strange and hostile land, after an initial religious thought—the recollection of a youth spent in a Christian home, or the repentance of a dying man—Napoleon expresses his dearest wish in the form of a prayer: to have his last resting place in the capital of that France over which he had once ruled supreme. Perhaps he had a premonition of what is today a reality: the endless procession that files past his tomb, which has become one of the great sights of the world.

By mentioning his second wife, Marie-Louise, in his will, and urging her in a codicil to supervise the execution of some of his last wishes, he shows himself able to forget the present and think only of the past. She it was who bore him a son, that "Prince of France" who grew up away from him in a foreign land and died a Frenchman haunted by the crushing burden of memory. It is to this son, this heir of whom he thinks increasingly, that he sends a condensed version of his political testament.

After certain well-known reflections upon persons and events, and even a justification of that much discussed decision which cost the Duke of Enghien his life, he thinks of his numerous family. Then come the various bequests and dispositions. Their quantity is impressive. How many names he mentions!

It is natural that he should think chiefly of his son. He leaves his heir, the king of Rome, his personal weapons and effects, everything he used in the campaigns which made him famous, his trophies, his books, his collections, his clothes. There is nothing dull about the long list which enumerates them; it is full of poetry and splendor. It is the last consolation of a dying man to think that Sobieski's saber, the sword of Austerlitz, Frederick the Great's Potsdam alarm clock, the blue cloak of Marengo, his saddles, his uniforms, his hats, his linen will go to the son whose birth was his greatest joy as a man, and who was the focus of all his pride and tenderness. He cannot imagine that Austria's iron hand will prevent the execution of his last pious wish, and he expresses the hope that all these souvenirs will be passed to his son "when he is sixteen years old." The refrain recurs five times in the will and its codicils. Is this not yet another sign of the extraordinary foresight of the exile of St. Helena? It would indeed be at that age that the Duke of Reichstadt, despite his archduke's upbringing and his estrangement from everything that made up his past, became aware of who he was and ought to be, making every effort to become worthy of his father's memory, until that piercing obsession made him succumb to the moral torments which were to complete his physical weakness. These personal effects, listed with such precision, were never to reach his son, who died too soon: they went to Madame Mère, who redistributed them among her own children.

The Empress Marie-Louise received only the lace and a little gold bracelet with Napoleon's hair, these modest gifts being quite enough for the fickle archduchess who replaced her unhappy exiled spouse so soon with a one-eyed general.

The members of the imperial family, for whom he had done so much in his times of glory and triumph, were not forgotten. Their descendants have set the greatest store by these relics; they guard them piously or have entrusted them to great institutions. Indeed when the occasion has presented itself some members have even bought relics back from the families of other beneficiaries.

But above all the emperor wished to express his gratitude to those who were with him during the six years of his exile, notably to those who remained true to the last, who suffered the isolation, climate and hardships of St. Helena with him. He rewarded the devotion of General Montholon, of Bertrand, his grand-marshal, of Marchand, his valet, forgetting no servant or member of his household. He even left a historic souvenir, a cameo given to him by the pope, to an Englishwoman, Lady Holland. She, like her husband, and unlike the race that had sought his destruction and obliteration, had taken pity upon the vanquished captive. The speeches of Lord Holland in the House of Lords had met with no response, but Lady

Holland sent books and parcels of wine and food from England.

Looking back beyond the sad ending of his life, he recalls his recent and glorious past, thinking of all those, soldiers and civilians, who have assisted him in his rise to glory and served him in the course of his fabulous career. The famous and the most insignificant and obscure are rewarded, and sometimes the bequest is accompanied by praise and tender recollections, and even in some cases by advice and injunctions. To the very end he continued to make political matches, giving instructions as to the future marriages of his numerous nephews and nieces. Moreover, he recommends the Duke of Istria to marry Duroc's daughter, in order to join by marriage the families of his two favorite marshals.

The Corsicans, and above all those who came to Elba, are not forgotten. Finally, from his civil list he grants pensions and important gifts to the wounded and to soldiers who fought in his glorious and less glorious campaigns. The list is a long one. From his remote island he is anxious to discharge what he believes to be a sacred debt. He has been their emperor; for them his image is identified with that of their country. Though himself in the depths of misfortune, he must do what he believes still to lie within his powers.

This, the emperor's last message, written sometimes in a noble, sometimes a familiar style, makes moving reading despite its lists of names and figures. Although the body is weakening, all Napoleon is still there: the warrior, the politician, the family man and, above all, the leader who is grateful for services rendered and is able to distinguish true devotion from a sham of feeling.

How different things would be eleven years later at the death of the son in whom the conqueror of Europe had placed all his hope. That penniless prince would leave no will. On his death there was merely a rapid distribution of the objects given him through the generosity of his mother and his grandfather the Austrian emperor. The final irony was that Metternich acquired two souvenirs of his prisoner, a little chain with medals, and an ornamental cane with a talisman. But the "Prince of France," brought up so far from his own land, had thought long and often over the printed texts of his illustrious father's will, and above all he had sensed its grandeur.

Indeed it may perhaps be in part this precious document which instilled in him the cult of remembrance which dominated the last years of his life. General Hartmann, who was asked about the tastes and habits of the luckless duke shortly after his death, described his filial feelings as follows: "As for the love he bore his father it suffices to say that he idolized him."

The emperor's will is the most important and enthralling of all his writings while on St. Helena, writings which make such a vital contribution to his history and legend. Written at the time when a dying man sees his whole life as one and makes his final assessments, it has the importance of a final souvenir and of piece of evidence crucial to the understanding of a man who, though he may have ended his life in exile and defeat, wished nevertheless to die as the great emperor he had once been.

SUZANNE D'HUART
Curator of the National Archives

NAPOLEON

This day April 15, 1821, at Longwood House upon the island of St. Helena. This is my last will and testament.

I

1. I die in the Apostolic and Roman faith, in whose bosom I was born more than fifty years ago.

2. I wish my ashes to rest beside the Seine, in the midst of the French nation I have loved so dearly.

3. I have always been well pleased with my most dear spouse Marie-Louise; to the last I retain the most tender feelings for her. I request her to watch over my son and to guard him against the pitfalls which have surrounded him since childhood.

4. I urge my son never to forget that he was born a French prince, and never to lend himself to the triumvirate which oppresses the people of Europe. In no way whatsoever is he to fight or harm France. He is to adopt my own device: *Tout pour le peuple français* [Everything for the French people].

5. I die before my time, murdered by the English oligarchy and its hired assassin. The people of England will avenge me all too soon.

6. The unhappy results of the two invasions of France, when she was still so rich in resources, are due to the treason of Marmont, Augereau, Talleyrand and Lafayette: I forgive them. May the posterity of France forgive them as I have done.

7. I thank my good and most excellent mother, the cardinal, my brothers Joseph, Lucien, Jérôme, Pauline, Caroline, Julie, Hortense, Catherine and Eugène for their enduring concern.

I forgive Louis the libel he published in 1820, full of false assertions and forged evidence.

Aujourd'hui 15 avril 1821 à Longwood île de Sainte Hélène

Ceci est mon testament, ou acte de ma dernière volonté

Je meurs dans [...] qui est celle de mes [pères] dans le sein de la
[...] depuis plus de cinquante ans.

Je désire que mes cendres reposent sur les bords de la Seine
au milieu de ce peuple français que j'ai tant aimé.

J'ai toujours eu à me louer de ma très chère épouse Marie-Louise
je lui conserve jusqu'au dernier moment les plus tendres
sentiments je la prie de veiller pour garantir mon fils des embûches
qui environnent encore son enfance.

Je recommande à mon fils de ne jamais oublier qu'il est
[né] prince français et de ne jamais se prêter à être un
instrument entre les mains des triumvirs qui [...]
[...] l'Europe — il ne doit jamais [...]
[...] manière [...] il doit [...]
[...] pour le peuple français

Je meurs prématurément assassiné par l'oligarchie
anglaise et son [salaire] le peuple anglais [...]
[...]

les 2 issus de [...] des [...]
[...] je [...]
[...]

[...]
[...]

Je remercie ma bonne et très excellente [...]
[...] mes frères [...]
[...] je pardonne [...]
[...]

8. I disown the *Manuscript of St. Helena* and the other works appearing under the title *Maxims and Opinions*, which people have seen fit to publish in the course of the last six years. Those are not the principles which have governed my life.

I had the Duke of Enghien arrested and condemned because it was necessary to the security, interest and honor of the French nation at a time when, as he admitted, the Count of Artois maintained sixty assassins in Paris. In like circumstances I would do as much again.

II

1. I leave to my son the boxes, decorations and other items such as silverware, camp bed, weapons, saddles, spurs, the sacred vessels of my chapel, books and linen which constitute my personal effects, according to the inventory attached, marked A. I wish him to hold this modest bequest dear, for it commemorates a father of whom he will hear the whole world speak.
2. I leave to Lady Holland the antique cameo which Pope Pius VI gave me in Tolentino.
3. I leave to Count Montholon two million francs as proof of my satisfaction with the filial devotion which he has displayed toward me for six years, and in order to compensate him for the losses which he has incurred through his sojourn on St. Helena.
4. I leave 500,000 francs to Count Bertrand.
5. I leave to Marchand, my head valet, 400,000 francs. The services which he has rendered have been those of a friend. I wish him to marry a widow, sister or daughter of an officer or soldier of my Old Guard.
6. To Saint-Denis, 100,000 francs.
7. To Noverraz, 100,000 francs.
8. To Pierron, 100,000 francs.
9. To Archambault, 50,000 francs.
10. To Coursot, 25,000 francs.
11. To Chandellier, *idem*.
12. To Abbé Vignali, 100,000 francs. I wish him to build his house near Pontenovo di Rostino.

de pièces falsifiées

Deuxieme
Ricxxxx

8° je désarme le monument de St hélène et autres ouvrages

des lettres de martins, dentaux que lui sira plus apostille legres

dans les désire pas les reyles qui ... deregrs en

vie j'ai fait arêter en juges le duc d'enghien.

necessaire a la surete a l'interest d'honneur du peuple francais lorsque

le duc ... ortes ... avoué ... depuis des

Semblable circunstance j'agirous de même

1° je legue a mon fils les bustes, ordres en autres objets tels

quargenterie du ... , armes, selles ... vases de ma

chapelle ... linges, ... qui me servir a mon usage et a

mon usage enfermé alétat ... et ... je désire

qu'ilte faible legue lui sire chère comme lui rt e laisse

le souvenir d'un père ... demoins lentendre

je legue a ... hollande le camé antique que ...

ma donné a toulon ...

je legue ou ... unethotin deux millions de francs

prennan de me satisfac ... des scleurs fideles

... rendu de ...

Son séjour a St hélène lui a occasioné

je legue au valet Bertrand cinq cent mille francs

je legue a marchand mon premier valet de chambre quatre

cent mille francs. Les services qu'il m'a rendu sont ...

... je désire qu'il epouse une veuve, sœur

ou fille d'un officier ou soldat de la vieille garde

idem a ... cent mille francs

idem a montrond cent mille francs

idem pierre cent mille francs

idem a archambault cinquante mille francs

9 idem a cursos vingt trois mille francs

idem a chalott idem

... l'autre vigoureux cent mille francs je désire

... j'ai été de montrand ... quinzieme des états

13. To Count Las Cases, 100,000 francs.

14. To Count Lavallette, 100,000 francs.

15. To Surgeon-in-Chief Larrey, 100,000 francs; he is the most virtuous man I have ever known.

16. To General Brayer, 100,000 francs.

17. To General Lefebvre-Desnouettes, 100,000 francs.

18. To General Drouot, 100,000 francs.

19. To General Cambronne, 100,000 francs.

20. To the children of General Mouton-Duvernet, 100,000 francs.

21. To the children of brave Labédoyère, 100,000 francs.

22. To the children of General Giraud, killed at Ligny, 100,000 francs.

23. To the children of General Chartrand, 100,000 francs.

24. To the children of virtuous General Travot, 100,000 francs.

25. To General Lallemand, sr., 100,000 francs.

26. To Count Réal, 100,000 francs.

27. To Costa, of Bastelica in Corsica, 100,000 francs.

28. To General Clausel, 100,000 francs.

29. To Baron Meneval, 100,000 francs.

30. To Arnault, the author of *Marius*, 100,000 francs.

31. To Colonel Marbot, 100,000 francs; I charge him to persist with his writing, guarding the glory of the armies of France and confounding their slanderers and apostates.

32. To Baron Bignon, 100,000 francs; I charge him to write the history of French diplomacy from 1792 to 1815.

troisième page

13° idem au comte Las Cases cent mille francs

14° idem au comte Lavalette cent mille francs

15 idem au chirurgien en chef Larrey cent mille francs. C'est l'homme le plus vertueux que j'aie connu

idem au général Brayer cent mille francs

idem au général Lefebvre-Desnouettes cent mille francs

idem au général Drouot cent mille francs

idem au général Cambronne cent mille francs

20 idem aux enfants du général Mouton-Duvernet cent mille francs

21 idem aux enfants du brave Labédoyère, cent mille francs

idem aux enfants du général Girard tué à Ligny cent mille francs

idem aux enfants du général Chartran cent mille francs

idem aux enfants du vertueux général Travot cent mille francs

idem au général Lallemand l'aîné cent mille francs

idem au comte Réal cent mille francs

idem à Costa de Bastelica en Corse cent mille francs

idem au général Clauzel cent mille francs

idem au baron de Menneval cent mille francs

30 idem à Arnault auteur de Marius cent mille francs

31 idem au colonel Marbot cent mille francs. Je l'engage à continuer à écrire pour la défense de la gloire des armées françaises et en confondre les calomniateurs et les apostats

32 idem au baron Bignon cent mille francs. Je l'engage à écrire l'histoire de la diplomatie française de 1792

33. To Poggi, of Talavo, 100,000 francs.

34. To Surgeon Emery, 100,000 francs.

35. These sums are to be drawn from the six millions which I deposited in Paris when I left in 1815, and from interest accruing at 5% since July 1815. The accounts should be verified by Counts Montholon and Bertrand, and Marchand.

36. Everything the investment may have yielded above the sum of 5,600,000 francs which has already been disposed of is to be distributed to the wounded of Waterloo and to the officers and men of the Elban batallion, according to a list to be drawn up by Montholon, Bertrand, Drouot, Cambronne and Surgeon Larrey.

37. In the event of death these bequests are to be paid to widows and children, or, if there are none, to be restored to the principal sum.

III

1. My private estate is my own property, and no French law has deprived me of it as far as I am aware. The treasurer, Baron de la Bouillerie, is to be asked to present its accounts. It must consist of more than 200 million francs, namely: 1. the portfolio containing the savings which I made for fourteen years from my civil list, which amounted to more than twelve million francs a year if I remember right; 2. the interest on the portfolio; 3. the furniture of my palaces as they were in 1814, including the palaces of Rome, Florence and Turin, all of which furniture was acquired by means of the revenues from the civil list; 4. the proceeds of the sale of my houses in the kingdom of Italy, such as silver, silverware, jewelry, furniture, stables. Prince Eugène and the royal intendant Campagnoni will produce the books.

2. I leave my private estate partly to the officers and men of the French army who fought from 1792 to 1815 for the glory and independence of the nation; the other half is to go to the towns and countryside of Alsace, Lorraine, Franche-Comté, Burgundy, the Ile de France, Champagne, Forez, and Dauphiné, which have all suffered on the occasion of one or the other invasion. One million is to go to the town of Brienne, and one million to the town of Méry.

I nominate Count Montholon, Count Bertrand and Marchand my executors.

This testament, written entirely in my own hand, is signed and sealed with my seal.

NAPOLEON

je legue mon domaine privé moitié aux officiers

et soldats qui restent de l'armée française qui ont combattu

depuis 1815 pour la gloire et l'indépendance de la nation

le partage sera fait au prorata des quittances d'acture

moitié aux villes et campagnes d'alsace, de lorraine

de franche-comté — de bourgogne, de l'île de france — de champagne

forêt dauphiné qui auraient souffert par l'une ou

l'autre invasion. il sera de cette somme prélevé un

million pour la ville de Brienne et un

million pour celle de Méry

je nomme le comte montholon, Bertrand et

Marchand mes exécuteurs testamentaires

ce présent testament tout écrit de ma

propre main est signé et scellé de mes armes

Napoléon

signé et paraphé pour nous président
du tribunal suivant notre procès
verbal de ce jour. Paris le vingt sept
mars 1853. Debelleyme

Vu rectifié à Tours 2ᵉ Bureau
le Vingt Sept Mars 1853. N° 39.
reçu un franc cinquante centime
et cinqte le même jour fº 30 ...
et rº x fº 31 ...
un cinq franc et cinquante centime
5 10 ...

Annexé à la minute d'un acte
de dépôt reçu par moi notaire à
Paris, soussigné, aujourd'hui vingt sept
mars mil huit cent cinquante trois

LIST (a)

1. None of the effects which I have used are to be sold; what is left over is to be shared between my executors and my brothers.
2. Marchand will preserve my hair and have it fashioned into bracelets, each with a little locket, to be sent to Empress Marie-Louise, to my mother, to each of my brothers, sisters, nephews and nieces, to the cardinal, and a more substantial one for my son.
3. Marchand is to send one of my pairs of golden shoe buckles to Prince Joseph.
4. A little pair of golden garter buckles to Prince Lucien.
5. A golden collar clasp to Prince Jérôme.

LIST (a)

Inventory of the Effects Marchand is to Keep and Pass on to my Son

1. My silver toilet case, the one on my table, with all its utensils, razors, etc.
2. My alarm clock; it is Frederick II's alarm clock, which I removed from Potsdam (in box no. III).
3. My two watches, one with the chain of the empress's hair and a chain of my own hair for the other one; Marchand is to have it made in Paris.
4. My two seals (the seal of France is in box no. III).
5. The little gilt clock now in my bedroom.
6. My washstand, its washbowl and support.
7. My bedside tables, the ones I used in France, and my silver-gilt bidet.
8. My two iron bedsteads, my mattresses and blankets, if they can be preserved.
9. My three silver brandy flasks, which my grooms carried in the field.
10. My French spyglass.
11. My spurs (two pairs).
12. Three ebony boxes, nos. I, II, III, containing my snuff boxes and other things.
13. A silver-gilt pan.

PERSONAL LINEN

6 shirts
6 handkerchiefs
6 cravats
6 napkins
6 pairs of silk hose
4 black collars
6 pairs of socks
2 pairs of batiste sheets
2 pillowcases
2 dressing gowns
2 pairs of nightclothes
1 pair of braces
4 pairs of white cashmere underpants and under-shirts
6 scarves
6 flannel vests
4 pairs of drawers
6 pairs of gloves
1 little box full of my snuff
1 gold collar clasp
1 pair of decorative gold buckles ⎱ in the little
1 pair of gold shoe buckles ⎰ box no. III

GARMENTS

1 chasseur's uniform
1 grenadier's uniform
1 national guardsman's uniform
2 hats
1 gray and green cloak
1 blue cloak (the one I wore at Marengo)

1° — Il ne sera vendu aucun des effets qui m'ont servi ; le surplus sera partagé entre mes exécuteurs testamentaires et mes frères.

2° — Marchand conservera mes cheveux, et en fera faire un bracelet avec un petit cadenas en or, pour être envoyé à l'Impératrice Marie Louise, à ma Mère et à chacun de mes frères, sœurs, neveux, nièces ; le Cardinal, et un plus considérable pour mon fils.

3° — Marchand enverra une de mes paires de boucles à souliers en or au Prince Joseph.

4° — Une petite paire de boucles en or à jarretière au prince Lucien.

5° — Une boucle de Col en or au Prince Jérôme.

Inventaire de mes effets que Marchand gardera pour remettre à mon fils.

1° — Mon nécessaire d'argent celui qui est sur ma table garni de tous ses ustensiles Rasoirs etc.

2° — Mon réveil matin, c'est le réveil matin de Frédéric II que j'ai pris à Potsdam (dans la boite N° ...)

3° — Mes deux montres avec la Chaine de Cheveux de l'Impératrice et une Chaine de mes Cheveux pour l'autre montre, Marchand le fera faire à Paris.

4° — Mes deux Sceaux (l'un ... renfermé dans la boite N° III)

5° — le petit pendule doré qui est actuellement dans ma Chambre à coucher

6° — Mes Lavabo, son pot à eau et son pied

7° — Mes table de nuit celle que mon service en fer ... et mon lit de Marengo

8° — Mes deux lits de fer, Mes matelas et mes couvertures s'ils se peuvent ...

9° — Mes ... flacons d'argent où l'on mettrait mon eau de vie que prendrait avec ... Champ de bataille

10° — Mes Lunettes de France

11° — Mes éperons deux paires

12° — trois boites d'acajou N° I. II. III. renfermant une tabatière

13° — Une ... à toilette
Linge à toilette.

6 — Chemises

6 — Mouchoirs

6 — Cravates

6 — Serviettes

6 — paires de bas de soie

4 — Cols Noirs

6 — paires de Chaussettes

2 — paires de Draps de batiste

2 — taies d'oreiller

2 — Robes de Chambre

2 — pantalons de Nuit

1 — paire de bretelles

4 — Calottes velles et Cotonnes Ll...

6 — Madras

6 — Gilets de flanelle

4 — Caleçons

6 — paires de ...

1 — petite boite pleine de mon tabac

1 — boucle de Col en or

1 — paire de boucles en jarretière en or } renfermés dans la petite boite N° III.

1 — paire de boucles en or à soulier

Habillement.

1 — Uniforme Chasseur

1 — d° Grenadier

1 — d° Garde nationale

2 — Chapeaux

1 — Capote grise et verte

1 — Manteau bleu (celui que ...)

1 little sable vest
2 pairs of shoes
1 pair of slippers
6 girdles

NAPOLEON

1 — Rébellion petite note.
2 — point de ...
2 — point de ...
1 — point de ...
6 — Contraval.

Napoléon

Annexée à la minute d'un acte de Dépôt
reçu par M.e Notaire à Paris, soussigné, aujourd'hui
vingt six mars mil huit cent cinquante trois.

Noël

Enregistré et paraphé au nom
Président du Tribunal selon
notre procès verbal de ce jour
Paris le vingt six mars 1853

Visé pour timbre à Paris 2.e Bureau le vingt six Mars 1853. N.º 39
reçu un franc cinquante centimes & enreg.t le même jour f.º N.º M.C.C.
reçu cinq francs & cinquante centimes ...

1 — 50
5 — 50
7 —

List Attached to my Will
Longwood, island of St. Helena, April 15, 1821

I
1. The sacred vessels used in my chapel at Longwood.
2. I entrust them to Abbé Vignali, who is to give them to my son when he is sixteen.

II
1. My weapons, namely: my sword, the one I carried at Austerlitz; Sobieski's saber; my dagger; my sword; my hunting knife, my two pairs of Versailles pistols.
2. My golden toilet case, which I used on the mornings of Ulm, Austerlitz, Jena, Eylau, Friedland, the island of Lobau, the Moscowa, Montmirail. It is for this reason that I want my son to hold it dear. Count Bertrand has had charge of it since 1814.
3. I charge Count Bertrand to care for and preserve these items and give them to my son when he is sixteen.

III
1. Three little ebony chests: the first contains thirty-three snuff boxes, or bonbonnieres; the second, twelve boxes with the imperial arms, two small spyglasses and four boxes found upon Louis XVIII's table in the Tuileries, March 20, 1815; the third, three snuff boxes decorated with silver medals, for the emperor's use, and sundry pieces of toiletry, according to the inventories numbered I, II and III.

2. My camp beds, which I used in all my campaigns.
3. My campaign telescope.
4. My silver toilet cases, one of each of my uniforms, a dozen shirts, and a complete set of each of my sets of clothes, and generally of everything I used for my toilet.
5. My washbasin.
6. A little clock which is in my bedchamber at Longwood.
7. My two watches, and the chain made of the empress's hair.
8. I charge Marchand, my head valet, to keep these items and give them to my son when he is sixteen.

IV
1. My collection of decorations.
2. My silverware and the Sèvres porcelain I have used on St. Helena (lists B and C).
3. I charge Count Montholon to keep these items and give them to my son when he is sixteen.

V
1. My three saddles and bridles, and the spurs I have used on St. Helena.
2. My five sporting guns.
3. I charge my huntsman Noverraz to keep these items and give them to my son when he is sixteen.

VI
1. Four hundred volumes selected from those I made most use of in my library.
2. I charge Saint-Denis to keep them and give them to my son when he is sixteen.

Longwood Isle de St. Hélène le 15 Avril 1821.

I

1° Les Vases sacrés qui ont servi à ma Chapelle à Longwood

2° Je charge l'abbé Vignaly de les garder et de les remettre à mon fils quand il aura seize ans.

II

1° Mes armes, savoir: Mon Épée, celle que je portais à Austerlitz; le sabre de Sobielsky; mon poignard, mon glaive; mon couteau de chasse mes deux paires de pistolets de Versailles.

2° Mon nécessaire d'or; celui qui m'a servi le matin d'Ulm, d'Austerlitz, d'Eylau, de Friedland, de l'Isle de Lobeau, de la Moscowa, et de Mont mirail; Sous ce point de vue je désire qu'il soit précieux à mon fils (Le Ct Bertrand en est déjà depuis 1814)

3° Je charge le Ct Bertrand de soigner et conserver ces objets et de les remettre à mon fils quand il aura seize ans.

III

1° Trois petites caisses d'acajou contenant la première trente trois tabatières bonbonnière, la deuxième douze boites aux armes impériales, dans cette la et quatre boites trouvées sur la table de Louis XVIII aux Thuileries le 20 Mars la troisième trois tabatières ornée de médailles d'argent à l'usage de l'... et Diverses effets de toilette conformément aux états numérotés I. II...

2° Mes lits de Camp dont j'ai fait usage dans toutes mes campagnes

3° Ma lunette de Guerre

4° Mon nécessaire de toilette, un de chacun de mes uniformes, une douzaine de ... et un objet complet de chacun de mes habillements et généralement de tout ce qui sert à ma toilette.

5° Mon Lavabo

6° Une petite pendule qui est dans ma Chambre à coucher de Longwood

7° Ma ... montre et la Chaine de Cheveux de l'Impératrice

8° Je charge Marchand mon premier valet de Chambre de garder ces objets et de les remettre à mon fils lorsqu'il aura seize ans.

IV

1° Mes médailles

2° Mon argenterie et ma porcelaine de Sèvres dont j'ai fait usage à St Hélène État (6 y 8)

3° Je charge le Ct Montholon de garder ces objets et de les remettre à mon fils quand il aura seize ans.

V

1° Mes 3 selles et Brides, mon éperons qui m'ont servi à St Hélène

2° Mes fusils de chasse au nombre de cinq

3° Je charge mon Chasseur Noverraz de garder ces objets et de les remettre à mon fils quand il aura seize ans.

VI

1° Quatre cent volumes choisis dans ma bibliothèque parmi ceux qui ont le plus servi à mon usage

2° Je charge St Denis de les garder et de les remettre à mon fils quand il aura seize ans.

Napoléon

LIST (B)
List of Effects which I left with the
Count of Turenne
Sobieski's saber (it is mentioned in list A by mistake: that is the saber carried by the emperor at Aboukir, which is in the hands of Count Bertrand).

1 great chain of the Légion d'Honneur
1 silver-gilt sword
1 consul's sword
1 iron sword
1 velvet sash
1 chain of the Golden Fleece
1 little steel dressing case
1 silver night light
1 hilt of an antique saber
1 Henri IV hat and my plume
The emperor's lace
1 little collection of medals
2 Turkish carpets
2 embroidered coats of crimson velvet, with vests and breeches

1. I give to my son: Sobieski's saber, the chain of the Légion d'Honneur, the silver-gilt sword, the consul's sword, the iron sword, the chain of the Golden Fleece, the Henri IV hat with plume, the golden toilet case for teeth, left at the dentist's.
2. To Empress Marie-Louise, my lace.
To Madame, the silver night light.
To the cardinal, the little steel toilet case.
To Prince Eugène, the silver-gilt candlestick.
To Princess Pauline, the little collection of medals.
To the queen of Naples, a little Turkish carpet.
To Queen Hortense, a little Turkish carpet.
To Prince Jérôme, the hilt of the antique saber.
To Prince Joseph, an embroidered coat, vest and breeches.
To Prince Lucien, an embroidered coat, vest and breeches.

NAPOLEON

Inventaire des effets que j'ai laissé chez Monsieur le Comte de Turenne.

1 Sabre de Sobieski (c'est pour...)
1 Grand Collier de la Légion d'honneur
1 Épée en vermeille
1 Glaive de Consul
1 Épée en fer
1 Ceinturon de velours
1 Collier de la toison d'or
1 petit nécessaire en cuivre
1 Vaisselle en argent
1 poignée de sabre antique
1 Chapeau et l'Étrivy or et mon..
les Dentelles de St Napoléon
1 petit médailler
2 tapis turc
2 Manteaux de velours cramoisy brodés avec vestes et culottes.

1 —   Je donne a Mon fils le sabre de Sobieski.
D°   1 Collier de la Légion d'honneur
D°   1 Épée en vermeille
D°   1 Glaive de Consul
D°   1 Épée en fer
D°   1 Collier de la toison d'or
D°   1 Chapeau — l'Étrivy et le tapis.
D°   les nécessaires d'or pour les dentelles de St...

2 —   a l'Impératrice Marie Louise   Mes Dentelles
a Madame   la vaisselle en argent
au Cardinal   le petit nécessaire en cuivre
au Prince Eugène   le ceinturon en vermeille
a la Princesse Pauline   le petit médailler
a la Reine de Naples   un petit tapis turc
a la Reine Hortense   un petit tapis turc
au Prince Jérôme   la poignée de sabre antique
au Prince Joseph   un Manteau brodé veste et culotte
au Prince Lucien   un Manteau brodé veste et Culotte.

Annexé à la minute d'un acte de
Dépôt reçu par moi Notaire à
Paris, soussigné, ce jourd'hui vingt —
six mars mil huit cent cinquante
trois

Noël

Signé comparant par
mon Président du
tribunal selon notre
procès verbal du
vingt six
six mars 1853

Napoléon

Enrégistré pour timbre à Paris 2e Bureau le vingt six Mars 1853 f° 39
reçu un franc cinquante centimes et Décimes le même jour
f. 31 d° C. 8 reçu cinq francs et cinquante centimes de...

1 50
5 50
7 —

This is my will, written entirely in my own hand.
NAPOLEON

Le Testament, les cinq codicilles et les deux lettres ci-après, ayant déposés jusqu'à ce jour aux archives de la cour de Canterbury, ont été remis ce jour seize 16 mars 1853 par M. le comte de Clarendon principal secrétaire d'état de S. M. B. à M. le Comte Colonna Walewski ambassadeur de S. M. l'Empereur Napoléon III près S. M. la Reine Victoria

En foi de quoi, j'ai signé ainsi que suit
fait à Londres le 16 mars 1853 —

A. Walewski

*Enregistré à Paris 2e Bureau le vingt six mars 1853 f° 92 M° c 9 x b
reçu deux francs le vingt cinquième de ce cent. décharge*
Jouable

ceci est mon testament
écrit tout entier de
ma propre main

Napoléon

Vignalis

CODICILS

April 16, 1821, Longwood
This is a codicil to my will.
1. I wish my ashes to rest beside the Seine, in the midst of the French people I have loved so dearly.
2. I leave to Counts Bertrand and Montholon and to Marchand the money, jewelry, silver, porcelain, furniture, books, weapons and in general everything that has belonged to me on the isle of St. Helena.
This codicil, written in my own hand, is signed and sealed with my seal.

NAPOLEON

avril le 16 — 1821 Longwood.   quinzième page

Ceci est un codicille de mon testament.

1° je désire que mes cendres reposent sur les bords
de la Seine au milieu de ce peuple
français que j'ai tant aimé

2°   je lègue au comte Bertrand, meubles
et marchand - argent, bijoux, argenterie
porcelaine, meuble, livres, armes et
et généralement tous ce qui m'appartient
dans l'île de St. Hélène

Ce codicille tout entier écrit de ma
main   est signé et scellé de mes armes

Napoléon

Annexé à la minute d'un
acte de dépôt reçu par moi
notaire à Paris, soussigné,
Aujourd'hui vingt six mars
mil huit cent cinquante trois

Noël

signé et parap[h]é par Monsieur
Président du tribunal, selon
notre procès verbal de ce jour
Paris, vingt six mars 1853.

Lebelleguic

Visé pour timbre à Paris 2.e Bureau le vingt six Mars 1853. №...
... sera ... cinquante centimes ... Enreg.é le même jour...
f. 31. ... ... cinq francs et cinquante centimes de ...

1 - 50
5 - 5
7 - "

Noël

This is a codicil to my will, written entirely in my own hand.

NAPOLEON

2

ceci est un deuxieme
codicile a mon testament
tout ecrit de ma propre
main

Napoleon

Bertrand
Vignali

AE I 13, n° 21 ½

April 24, 1821, Longwood.
This is my codicil, or the expression of my last will. From the liquidation of my Italian civil list, including money, jewels, silver, linen, furniture, stables, entrusted to the viceroy and which belongs to me, I have two millions available, which I leave to my most faithful servants. I hope that my son Eugène Napoleon will discharge the obligation without question; he cannot forget the forty millions I gave him, partly in Italy, partly as his share of his mother's inheritance.

1. Out of these two millions I leave Count Bertrand 300,000 francs, of which he will place 100,000 in the treasurer's account to be used according to my dispositions as the bequests of conscience.

2. To Count Montholon, 200,000 francs, of which he will assign 100,000 francs to the account for the same purpose.

ce 16 avril 1821 Longwood

ceci est mon codicille ou acte de ma dernière
volonté.

Sur la liquidation de ma liste civile d'Italie
tel que argent, bijoux, argenterie, linge
meubles, écurie dont le Vice roi est dépositaire
ainsi que ma particulier, je dispose de deux
millions que je lègue aux plus fidèles
serviteurs. j'espère que sans aucune
raison manifeste mon fils Ayant hérité les acquittera
fidèlement et ne pour oublie les 4,000,000
que je laissai dans six en Italie six ans
le partage de la succession de Sa mère.

1° Sur ces 2 millions je lègue au comte Bertrand
300,000 dont il versera 100,000 dans
la caisse du trésorier pour être employé
selon mes dispositions aux legs de
legs de conscience

2° au comte Montholon deux cent
mille. Dont il versera — en —
caisse pour — usage que ce —

3. To Count Las Cases, 200,000 francs, of which he will assign 50,000 to the account for the same purpose.

4. To Marchand, 100,000 francs, of which he will assign 50,000 to the account for the same purpose.

5. To Count Lavallette, 100,000 francs.

6. To General Hogendorp, the Dutchman, my aide-de-camp who has fled to Brazil, 100,000 francs.

7. To my aide-de-camp Corbineau, 50,000 francs.

8. To my aide-de-camp Caffarelli, 50,000 francs.

9. To my aide-de-camp Dejean, 50,000 francs.

10. To Percy, surgeon-in-chief at Waterloo, 50,000 francs.

11. 50,000 francs as follows: 10,000 to Pierron, the head of my household; 10,000 to Saint-Denis, my head huntsman; 10,000 to Noverraz; 10,000 to Coursot, head of my kitchens; 10,000 to Archambault, my outrider.

12. To Baron Meneval, 50,000 francs.

3.⁰ au comte Lascas 200,000 dont il versera
100,000 dans la caisse pour le même
usage que ci-dessus

4.⁰ à marchand 100,000 dont il
versera 50,000 à la caisse pour
le même usage que ci-dessus

5.⁰ au comte la Valette 100,000

6. augment ho gendant... mille
aide de camp Regnier au Brésil
100 000.

7.⁰ à mon aide de camp Atheman
50, 000

8. à mon aide de camp Gatinelly... ...,000
cinquante mille francs

9. à mon aide de camp Dejean 50 000

10 à perry Chevaylier en chef... ...
50, 000

11.⁰ 50, 000 Savary 50, 000 à pierre... mon
maître d'hôtel 50, 000 ci-dessus
mon premier chellen 10, 000 à
... 30, 000 à ... mon
maître d'hôtel 10, 000 à
... mon ...

12. au baron... 50 000

13. To the Duke of Istria, son of Bessières, 50,000 francs.

14. To Duroc's daughter, 50,000 francs.

15. To Labédoyère's children, 50,000 francs.

16. To the children of Mouton-Duvernet, 50,000 francs.

17. To the children of the brave and virtuous General Travot, 50,000 francs.

18. To Chartrand's children, 50,000 francs.

19. To General Cambronne, 50,000 francs.

20. To General Lefebvre-Desnouettes, 50,000 francs.

21. To be distributed to exiles wandering abroad, French, Italians, Belgians, Dutch or Spaniards, or from the Rhineland, at my executors' discretion, 100,000 francs.

22. To be distributed amongst those who lost limbs or were severely wounded at Ligny and Waterloo who are still alive, according to lists drawn up by my executors together with Cambronne, Larrey, Percy and Emery, 200,000 francs (the Guard will get double rates, the Elbans quadruple).

13 — au duc d'Istrie fils de bessieres — 50, 000
cinquante mille francs

14 — à la fille de duroc 50, 000 cinquante
mille francs

15 — aux enfants de la bedoyere 50, 000

16 — aux enfants de mouton duvernet
50, 000

17° — aux enfants du brave et vertueux général
Travaux 50, 000

18 — aux enfants de chartrand 50, 000

19 — au général Cambronne 50, 000

20 — au général lefevre desnouettes 50, 000

21 — pour etre repartis entre les proscrits
qui errent en pays étrangers françois ou
italiens, ou belges ou hollandois ou espagnols
ordres d'exécuteurs testamentaires 100, 000

22 — pour etre repartis entre les émigrés
ou blessés glorieusement de la grande armée
encore vivans sur des etats drelles
par mes exécuteur testamentaire j'auquelle
seront adjoints cambronne larrey percy
et Emmery et leur donne l'oubliant la
garde quatre ans alaunde lalelle
200, 000 deux cent mille francs

This codicil is written in my own hand and signed and sealed with my seal.

NAPOLEON

Vingt cinque
Delacroix

Ce codicille est écrit en entier de ma
propre main signé et scellé de
mes armes

Napoléon

Signé et paraphé par Mons.   Annexé à la minute d'un acte
Président du tribunal pour   de dépôt reçu par moi Notaire
notre procès verbal ce jour   à Paris. Soussigné, aujourd'hui
soir vingt six mars 1853   vingt six mars mil huit cent
        Delacroix   cinquante trois /

                                                    Noël

Visé pour timbre à Paris 9e Bureau le vingt six Mars 1853. N° 39.
reçu un franc cinquante centimes de l'enregistré le même jour f. 91
V° C° por 2e P. 41 A P. reçu cinq francs et cinquante centimes
de dixième

        1 - 50
        5 - 50
       ――――
        7 - ―

This is my codicil, or the last expression of my will. I urge my son Eugène Napoleon to carry it out exactly. It is all written in my own hand.

NAPOLEON

Ceci est mon codicille ou
acte de dernière volonté
dont je recommande la stricte
exécution à mes fils

Eugène Beauharnais
Cet écrit tout de

Mon propre main
Napoléon

April 24, 1821, Longwood.
This is a third codicil to my will of April 15.

1. Among the crown diamonds restored in 1814 there are five worth 600,000 francs each which were not crown property, but were part of my private fortune. They are to be included in my estate.

2. The banker Torlonia of Rome held two letters of credit of mine, each worth 300,000 francs, the product of my income from the island of Elba. Some time since 1815 Peyrusse, although he was not my treasurer and had no authority, has withdrawn this sum for his own benefit. He must be made to return it.

3. I leave to the Duke of Istria 300,000 francs, of which only 100,000 should go to the widow if the Duke is dead at the time of my will's execution. If there are no objections, I wish the duke to marry Duroc's daughter.

4. I leave to the Duchess of Frioul, Duroc's daughter, 200,000 francs; if she should die before the execution of my will, the mother is to receive nothing.

5. I leave to General Rigoud, the one who was exiled, 100,000 francs.

6. I leave to Boinod, pay commissioner, 100,000 francs.

7. I leave to the children of General Latort, killed at . . . in the 1815 campaign, 100,000 francs.

8. These 800,000 francs should be considered as added to the end of article 35 of my will, which will bring the sum of my legacies left in my will to 6,400,000 francs, excluding the gifts made in my second codicil.

ce 24 avril 1821 a longwood

ceci est un troisieme codicille a mon testament du
15 avril

1° parmis les diamant de la couronne qui furent remis
en 1814 il s'en trouve pour 300.000 * qui n'en etoit
pas et faisoit partie de mon avoir particulier
on les fera rentrer pour aquitter mes legues

2° j'avois chez le banquier ... de Rome
2 ou ... en lettres ... chargé ...
... revenu de ... dette . depuis 1815
le sieur de la ... qui qu'il ...
plus mon thresorier ne ... pas de caractere
a tire obligé cette somme on le lui fera
restituer

3° je legue au duc d'Istrie trois cent mille fr
dont ... cent mille franc ...
... mort leg ... je desire si ...
je legue au ...

4° mille franc fille de ... sieck dos vert
... de ligne il ne sera rien donné ...

5° je legue au general Rigaud celui qui ...
present cent mille fra

6° je legue a Boinod ... ...
cent mille franc

7° je legue aux enfants du general ...
tué a dans la campagne de 1813
cent mille francs

8° les 300.000 * de ligues seront ...
fils etoient porté ... de l'article
36° de ... testament ce qui portera
a 6.400.000 la somme des legues fait

This is written in my own hand, signed and sealed with my seal.

NAPOLEON

J'ai disposé par mon testament ... ...
les donations faites par mon second codicille,
ceci est écrit de ma propre main signé et
scellé de mes armes

Napoleon

Annexé à la minute d'un acte de dépôt
reçu par mon Notaire à Paris soussigné
aujourd'hui vingt six mars mil huit cent
cinquante trois /

... ...
... ... du tribunal ...
... procès verbal de ce jour
Paris vingt six mars 1853

Noël

... ... le vingt six Mars 1853.
...

This is the third codicil to my will, all written in my own hand, signed and sealed with my seal.

It shall be opened on the same day as, and immediately after, the opening of my will.

NAPOLEON

April 24, 1821, Longwood

This is a fourth codicil to my will. The dispositions which have been already made do not fulfill all our obligations; this has moved us to draw up a fourth codicil.

1. We leave to the son or grandson of Baron du Theil, lieutenant-general of artillery, once seigneur of Saint-André, who commanded the school of Auxonne before the Revolution, the sum of 100,000 francs as a token of our gratitude for the care which the brave general took of us when we were, as lieutenant and captain, under his command.

2. As much to the son or grandson of General Dugommier, who was commander-in-chief of the army at Toulon; it was under his command that we directed the siege and commanded the artillery; it is a testimonial to our recollection of the esteem, affection and friendship which that brave and fearless general displayed toward us.

3. Similarly we leave 100,000 francs to the son or grandson of Gasparin, deputy of the Convention, who represented the people at the army of Toulon, for having protected and authorized the plan

ceci est un quatrième codicile a mon testament
par les dispositions que nous avons faites précédent
n'ont pas rempli toutes nos obligations ce
que nous décide a faire ce quatrième codicile

1° nous léguons au fils ou petits fils du baron du Theil
lieutenant général d'artillerie ancien seigneur de
St André qui a commandé l'école d'auxonne
avant la révolution la somme de cent mille
cent mille francs comme souvenir de reconnaissance
pour les soins que ce brave général pris de nous
lorsque nous étions... lieutenant et capitaine sous
ses ordres

2° item au fils ou petits fils du général Dugommier
qui a commandé en chef l'armée de toulon
somme de cent mille francs (100,000) nous avons
sous les ordres dirigés ce siège ... l'infanterie
avec un témoignage de souvenir pour les marques
d'estime, d'affection et d'amitié que nous a
donné cet brave et intrépide général

3° item nous léguons cent mille francs
(100,000) aux fils ou petit fils du
député a la convention gasparin
représentant du peuple a l'armée de
toulon pour avoir protégé et
sanctionné de son autorité le

which we submitted, which took the town and which was contrary to that sent by the Committee of Public Safety. With his protection Gasparin shielded us from the persecution of the ignorant general staff commanding the army before the arrival of my friend Dugommier.

4. Likewise we leave 100,000 francs to the widow, son or grandson of our aide-de-camp Muiron, killed at our side at Arcola, covering us with his body.

5. Likewise we leave 100,000 francs to N.C.O. Cantillon, who was tried for having sought the murder of the Duke of Wellington and found not guilty. Cantillon had as much right to kill that oligarch as the latter had to send me to die on the rock of St. Helena. Wellington, who conceived this murderous plot, sought to justify it as being in the interests of Great Britain. Cantillon, had he really assassinated the duke, would have been similarly justified by France's need to dispose of a general who had, moreover, violated the Peace of Paris and thereby rendered himself responsible for the blood of martyrs Ney, Labédoyère, etc., and for the crime of pillaging museums, contrary to the spirit of the treaties.

que nous avons donnés qui ___ la prise de cette p___
et qui était contraire ___ lui envoyé par le
comité de salut publique. _____ nous
a mis par sa protection à l'abri des persécuteurs
et la jouissance des états _____ qui commencèrent à
_____ avant l'arrivée de mon ami Duroc

4°. ___ nous léguons cent mille francs (_____)
à la veuve _____ petits fils de _____ qui de ___
coup _____ tué après avoir été _____
nous _____ de son corps

___ (10,000) dix mille francs au sous-officier
Cantillon qui a ___ un procès comme prévenu
d'avoir voulu assassiner lord Wellington et
dont il a été déclaré innocent — ___
avait autant de droit d'assassiner cet oligarque
que celui de ___ pour y périr sur les
rochers de Ste Hélène Wellington qui a proposé
cet _____ cherché à _____ sur tout
de la grande Bretagne, Cantillon s'il l'avait
___ le lord se serait _____
aurait été justifié par les mêmes motifs
_____ de la France de se défaire d'un
général qui d'ailleurs avait violé la
capitulation de Paris en _____

6. These 410,000 francs shall be added to the 6,400,000 francs we have bequeathed, bringing our bequests to 6,810,000 francs. These 410,000 francs should be taken as part of our will, article 35, and should be treated as our other bequests in every respect.

7. The £9,000 sterling we gave to Count and Countess Montholon should, if properly paid, be counted against the legacies we left them in our will; if not, the letters of credit are to be cancelled.

8. In view of the bequest to Count Montholon, the pension of 20,000 francs granted his wife is cancelled; the count is to pay it himself.

9. The administration of such an inheritance up to its final execution necessitates administrative and legal expenses, and we therefore authorize our executors to take 3% of the bequests, both from the 6,810,000 francs and the sums in the codicils, and the 200 millions of our private estate.

...pourelles du sang des martyrs ... la ...
... davier ... les musées ...
...

5. ... quatre cent mille francs seront ... au ... mais avons ... et ... légués au ... cés ... doivent être ... comme faisant partie de notre testament article III en suivre ... le même ... que les autres legues

7. Les ... sterling que nous avons donné au ... absolue ... doivent s'ils ont été ... être déduit et porté en ... sur les legues que nous ... faisons par nos testaments ... nous ... acquitté ... ...

8. ... lègue ... fait par notre testament au ... ... de sa femme elle ... l'administration d'une pareille succession jusqu'à ... legataire ... les frais de bureau, de ... démission de ... de plusieurs nos ... que nos exécuteurs testamentaire retiendront trois pour cent sur tous les legues soit sur les ... soit sur les sommes portées dans les ...

10. The sums accruing from these retentions are to be placed in the hands of a paymaster, and spent according to the requirements of our executors.

11. If the sums in question do not suffice to cover the costs, these shall be met by the three executors and the paymaster, each in proportion to the amount of the bequests we have made to them in our will and codicils.

12. If the sums in question are in excess of requirements, the balance will be divided *pro rata* among our three executors and our paymaster.

13. We name as paymaster Count Las Cases; and, failing him, his son; failing whom, General Drouot.

This codicil is written in our own hand, signed and sealed with our seal.

NAPOLEON

10. Les sommes provenant de ces [...] seront
déposées dans les mains d'un trésorier et [...]
sur mandat de mes exécuteurs testamentaires

11. Si les sommes provenant des dites [...] n'étaient pas
suffisantes pour pourvoir aux frais il y sera
pourvu au dépens de mes exécuteurs
testamentaires et du trésorier chacun dans
la proportion du legs que [...] leur aura
fait par mon testament ou codicille

12. Si les sommes provenant des susdites
[...] sont au dessus du besoin le surplus sera
partagé [...] mes trois exécuteurs testamentaires
et le trésorier dans le [...] de leur legs
respectifs

13. [...] le Ci [...] et à son défaut son fils et à défaut [...]
[...] trésorier [...]
ce présent codicille est entièrement écrit de ma
main, signé et scellé dans mes armes

Napoléon

EMPIRE FRANÇAIS
DIRECTION GÉNÉRALE
DES
ARCHIVES.

signé et paraphé par nous
Président du tribunal selon
notre procès-verbal de ce jour
à Paris le vingt six mars 1853.
Delessayne

Annexé à la minute d'inventaire
de dépôt reçu par moi notaire à
Paris [...] vingt six
[...] mil huit cent cinquante trois [...]
Noël

Vu pour timbre à Paris Dr. B[...]
le vingt six mars 1853. [...] 39
Reçu un franc cinquante centime
Et enreg[istré] le même jour [...]
C. g[...] [...] f. 32 [...]
Reçu cinq francs et cinquante
centime en tout
1.50
5.50
7.—

April 24, 1821, Longwood.
This is my codicil, or the expression of my last wishes.

From the sum in gold granted at Orléans in 1814 to Empress Marie-Louise, my most dear and beloved spouse, she owes me two millions, which I dispose of in the present codicil, in order to reward my faithful servants whom I commend to the protection of my dear Marie-Louise.

1. I recommended that the empress restore to Count Bertrand the income of 300,000 francs which he enjoyed in the duchy of Parma from Mount Napoleon and Milan, together with the arrears.

2. I urge her to do as much for the Duke of Istria, Duroc's daughter and other persons who served me faithfully and are still dear to me; she knows them.

3. Of the two millions mentioned I leave 300,000 francs to Count Bertrand. He will assign 100,000 of them to the paymaster's account to be used for legacies of conscience.

ce 24 avril 1821 Longwood

ceci est mon codicile ou acte de ma dernière
volonté

Sur les fonds remis en or à l'impératrice Marie Louise
ma très chère et bien aimée épouse à Orléans
en 1814 elle reste redevable deux millions dont
je dispose par le présent codicile enfin de
récompenser mes plus fidèles serviteurs
que je recommande du reste à la protection de
Madame Marie Louise

je recommande à l'impératrice de faire restituer au
comte Bertrand les 3 ou 400 mille francs de rente qui lui sont dues
dans le duché de parme et sur le mont Napoléon
de milan   ainsi que les arrérages échus

2°   je lui fais la même recommandation pour le duc d'Istrie
la fille de Duroc et autres de mes serviteurs
qui me sont restés fidèles et qui me sont
toujours chers . elle les connaît

3°   je lègue sur les deux millions ci dessus
Mentionnés trois cent mille francs au comte
Bertrand sur lesquels il versera 100, ou
dans la caisse du trésorier pour être employé
selon mes dispositions aux legues de Lucciana

4. I leave 200,000 francs to Count Montholon, of which 100,000 should be assigned to my pay-master's account for like use.

5. 200,000 francs to Count Las Cases, 100,000 to be assigned to the paymaster's account for like use.

6. 100,000 francs to Marchand, of which 50,000 are to be assigned to the paymaster's account for like use.

7. To Jean-Jérôme Levie, mayor of Ajaccio at the beginning of the revolution, or his widow, children or grandchildren, 100,000 francs.

8. To Duroc's daughter, 100,000 francs.

9. To the son of Bessières, Duke of Istria, 100,000 francs.

10. To General Drouot, 100,000 francs.

11. To Count Lavallette 100,000 francs.

12. Similarly, 100,000 francs as follows: 25,000 to Pierron, the head of my household; 25,000 to Noverraz, my huntsman; 25,000 to Saint-Denis, my librarian; 25,000 to Santini, my old usher.

13. Likewise, 100,000 francs as follows: 40,000 to Planat, artillery officer;

4º   je legue 200.000 au comte mathot sur les
quelles il versera 100.000 dans la caisse des
Hosiciens pour le meme — usage que ci
dessus

5º   idem 200,000 au comte ladlas sur les
quelles il versera 100,000 dans la caisse
des hosiciens pour le meme — usage
que ci dessus

6º   idem a marchand 100,000 sur les
quelles il versera 50,000 dans la caisse
pour le meme usage que ci dessus

7º   au comte depuis au commun de la pour tout ... petit
j'avoue le ... en autre remise enfants a petit
enfants 100,000

8º   a la fille des duroc 100,000

9º   au fils de Bessiere Sou distale 100.000

10. au general Drouot sur, 000

11º au comte lavalette 100.000

12º idem 100,000 savoir 25,000 a jeune mon
maitre d'hotel 25,000 a theurre
mon chasseur 25,000 a st denis. le
garde de mes livres 25,000
a s. hilaire mon valet de chambre

item 100,000 Savoir 40,000 a planat
mon officier d'ordonnance

20,000 to Hébert, recently a concierge at Rambouillet, who was part of my household in Egypt; 20,000 to Lavigne, recently in charge of one of my stables, who was my outrider in Egypt; 20,000 to Jannet-Dervieux, who was an outrider of my stables and who served me in Egypt.

14. 200,000 francs to be distributed in gifts to the inhabitants of Brienne-le-Château, who suffered the most.

15. The remaining 300,000 francs shall be distributed to the officers and men of the battalion of my Elban Guard who are still alive, or to their widows and children, according to the scale of their pay and the sums to be specified by my executors. Those who have lost limbs or who have been severely wounded to receive double. Their list is to be drawn up by Larrey and Emery.

This codicil is written entirely in my own hand, and signed and sealed with my seal.

NAPOLEON

20° vve Chebert demeurement écrite[?] a
Chantrotte[?] en qu'était de machandre
en Egypte 20° vve alexique qui était
demeurment par[?]loye[?] d'une de mes lunes
[?]qui était [?] piqueur en Egypto
De vve   ajavet desreurs que était pique
deslunes et meservie en Egypto

14°   deuve cent mille francs, seront distribue en aumone
      aux habitors de Brienne lectet[?] au qui vu le plus lorsa[?]

15°   les trois cent mille francs restant seront
      distribues aux offours et soldats du
      Batallon de ma garde d'elite selle
      actuelment vivave, ou a leur veuve
      evenfants   au prorates des apportents
      eu selon l'état quisera aneté par mes
      executeurs testauml. les aqutes vedtte
      graivement aurout double l'état kedera
      aneté par larey et Emmons

ce codicile est écrit tout en[?] de ma poere[?]
Maill signe et selle de mes armes

[signature]

Vite pour timbre à Paris 2° Beau le [?]
le[?] Mars 1853 [?] reçu un franc
cinquante centieme de curage à même jour
p. 39. 1b. c. f. 6. 7. 8. a 9.
      reçu cinq francs et cinquante centieme
de 10° [?]   1.50
              5.50
              7—

This is my codicil, or the expression of my last wishes. I charge my dearest spouse Empress Marie-Louise with its execution.

NAPOLEON

quarante huit pag.
[illegible]

Signé et paraphé par nous [illegible]
du tribunal suivant notre procès verbal
de ce jour. Paris le vingt six mars
1854 [illegible]

Annexé à la minute d'un acte de dépôt
reçu par le Notaire à Paris soussigné
aujourd'hui vingt six mars mil huit cent
cinquante [illegible]

[signature]

[illegible] est mon adroite en
[illegible]
[illegible]
[illegible]
[illegible] Marie Louise

[signature Napoléon]

Berthier

Vignali

Marchand

LETTERS

Monsieur Laffitte, in 1815 I deposited with you at the time of my departure from Paris a sum close to six millions, for which you gave me two copies of a receipt. I have cancelled one of them and I charge Count Montholon to present you with the other, in order that you should hand over to him after my death the sum in question, together with interest accrued at 5% from July 1, 1815, less the payments you have been charged to make in accordance with my instructions. I wish the liquidation of my account to be established only by yourself, Count Montholon, Count Bertrand and M. Marchand, and when this is done I grant you, by virtue of this present letter, entire and total discharge of the sum in question.

I have also deposited with you a box containing my collection of medals; would you please give it to Count Montholon.

Since this letter has no other object, I pray to God, Monsieur Laffitte, that He should keep you in His holy and worthy guard.

NAPOLEON

Longwood, island of St. Helena, April 15, 1821.

Monsieur Laffitte je vous ai remis en 1815 au moment de mon départ de Paris une somme de près de six millions dont vous m'avez donné Un Double reçu. J'ai annulé un des reçus et je charge le Comte de Montholon de vous présenter l'autre reçu pour que vous ayez à lui remettre après ma mort la dite somme avec les intérêts à raison de cinq pour cent à dater du premier juillet 1815 en défalquant les payements dont vous avez été Chargé en vertu d'ordres de moi.

Je désire que la liquidation de votre compte soit arrêtée d'accord entre vous le Comte Montholon, le Comte Bertrand et le sieur Marchand et cette liquidation réglée je vous donne par la présente décharge entière et absolue de la dite somme.

Je vous ai également remis une boîte contenant mes M. Juillet je vous prie de la remettre au Comte Montholon

Cette lettre n'étant à autre fin je prie Dieu Monsieur Laffitte qu'il vous ait en sa sainte et digne garde

Longwood Isle St Hélène le 25 avril 1821

Napoléon

Monsieur Baron de la Bouillerie, treasurer of my private estate, I request you after my death to pass the accounts and the balance to Count Montholon, whom I have asked to be the executor of my will.

Since this letter has no other object, I pray to God, Monsieur Baron de la Bouillerie, that He should keep you in His holy and worthy guard.

NAPOLEON

Longwood, island of St. Helena, April 25, 1821.

Monsieur le Baron Labouillerie Trésorier de
mon Domaine prière je vous prie d'en remettre le compte
et le montant après ma mort au Comte Montholon
que j'ai chargé de l'exécution de mon Testament

Cette lettre n'étant à autre fin je prie Dieu
Monsieur le Baron Labouillerie qu'il vous ait en
sa Sainte et Digne garde

Longwood Isle St. Hélène le 25 avril 1821

Signé et paraphé par nous
Président du tribunal selon
notre procès verbal de ce jour
ici le vingt sept mars 1853

$$\frac{7 - 70}{9 - 90}$$

SECOND CODICIL

April 16, 1821, Longwood.
This is a second codicil to my will.

By my first codicil of this day I gave everything belonging to me on this island of St. Helena to Count Bertrand, Count Montholon and Marchand. It was a device to foil the English. I wish my effects to be disposed of as follows:

1. There will be found 300,000 francs in silver and gold, of which 30,000 shall be assigned to the payment of my servants. The remainder shall be distributed as follows: 50,000 to Bertrand; 50,000 to Montholon; 50,000 to Marchand; 15,000 to Saint-Denis; 15,000 to Noverraz; 15,000 to Pierron; 15,000 to Vignali; 10,000 to Archambault; 10,000 to Coursot; 5,000 to Chandellier. The remainder shall be distributed in tips to the English doctors, Chinese servants and the parish precentor.

2. I leave to Marchand my diamond necklace.

3. I leave to my son all the effects which I have used, according to list A, attached.

4. All the rest of my effects are to be shared between Montholon, Bertrand and Marchand, and I forbid the sale of anything which has served my body.

avril ce 16 1821 Longwood Sage-première ... XXXXXXXXXXX, 5 avr. 8 h

ceci est un second codicile a mon testament
par moi premier codicile de ce jour — j'ai fait
donation de tout ce qui m'appartient dans l'ile de
St hélène aux G[énéraux] Bertrand, Montholon et Marchand
ceci uniquement pour mettre hors de cause les
anglais. Ma volonté est qu'il soit disposé de mes effets
de la manière suivante.

1° on trouvera 3[00?], 000 francs chargés
desquelles seront distrait 3[00?] 000 pour payer les
derniers de mes domestiques. Le restant sera
distribué 3[00?] 000 a Bertrand 250 000 a Montholon
300 000 a Marchand 15 000 a Saint Denis 15 000 a Noverraz
15 000 a Pieron 15 000 a Archambeau 10 000 a
Archambeau jn 10 000 a Coursot. Son autre [?]
Le reste sera distribué en gratification aux médecins
anglais. domestiques, chevaux et en charité à la
paroisse

2° je legue a marchand mon allen de
diamant

3° je legue a mon fils tous les effets qui sont
de a mon usage conformément à l'état ci joint

(a)
tout le reste de mes effets serra partagé entre
Bertrand Montholon Marchand de façon
qu'il n'en soit rien vendu de ce qui...

5. I leave to Madame, my most good and dear mother, the busts, frames and little pictures which are in my rooms, and the sixteen silver eagles, which she shall distribute among my brothers, sisters, nephews (Coursot is to carry these objects to her in Rome), together with the chains and necklaces from China which Marchand will give her, for Pauline.

6. All the legacies contained in this codicil are independent of those made in my will.

7. My will is to be opened in Europe, in the presence of those persons who have placed their signatures upon this envelope.

8. I name as my executors Count Montholon, Count Bertrand and Marchand. This codicil is all written in my own hand, and is signed and sealed with my seal.

servir à mon corps.   page dernière et dernière

§ 5e Je lègue à madame ma très bonne et chère
mère les bustes, quadres, petits tableaux qui sont dans
ma chambre, et les 16 aigles d'argent
distribuer entre mes frères, sœurs, neveux
je charge l'exécuteur de lui faire
les objets qu'une   aussi que les chaînes
collier de la Chine que marchand lui remettre
toutes les dernières contenues dans la
6e cédule j'une indépendante de cette
faite par mon testament.

7e l'ouverture de mon testament sera
faite en Europe en présence des personnes
qui ont signé dans l'enveloppe

8 j'institue mes exécuteurs testamentaires
les C. Montholon. Bertrand et marchand

Ce cédule tout écrit de ma propre main
et scellé de mes armes

Napoléon

signé et paraphé au désir de notre
procès verbal de ce jour. Paris le
vingt trois juin 1853

This is a second codicil to my will, all written in my own hand.

NAPOLEON

2

ceci est mon dernier
codicile a mon testant
tout écrit de ma propre
main

Napoléon

Bertrand
Vignali

AE I 13 n°21 ½

INSTRUCTIONS TO MY EXECUTORS

April 26, 1821, Longwood.
1. I wish all my legacies to be paid in full.
2. The 5,280,000 francs which I deposited with the banker Laffitte should have produced by January 1822, counting interest at 5% as I told him, some seven million francs. If there is any trouble the accounts must be verified at every level, since forces beyond my control have prevented me from writing and disposing of my funds. There must be no compromise on this point.
3. To my knowledge the banker Laffitte has only paid out the following sums on my account: 1. 20,000 francs to General Lallemand, sr.; 2. 3,000 francs to Gillis, my valet; 3. 100,000 francs to Count Las Cases; 4. 72,000 francs to Balcombe, on a letter of credit of Count Bertrand's; 5. an authorization, sent via Prince Eugène, to supply 12,000 francs per month from 1817, in London, for my own needs. The sum has not been forthcoming, except for a part with Messrs. Parker, which means that I owe Count Bertrand considerable sums, sums which must be reimbursed at once. As a result the winding up of my account with Laffitte should come to the total of 6,200,000 francs, capital and interest, or thereabouts, as of January 1, 1822.
4. The matter of my private estate is a matter of considerable importance and will give rise to much debate; but the return of Peyrusse's money, which was, I believe, paid to the crown; the liquidation of my Italian civil list, which should bring me several millions; the restoration of furniture now with the crown, which belonged to me before the existence of my civil list at the time of the consulate, and even when I was a general (the former being all the furniture of Saint-Cloud, and a part of that of the Tuileries, the latter a major part of the furniture of Rambouillet); the presents received either from rulers, or from the city of Paris, such as the fine malachite furnishings from Russia, the chandeliers, crystal glassware, and golden dinner service from the city of Paris: all these raise special and particular issues. These various objects must have a value that amounts to several millions.
5. As for all the crown furniture which belongs to me, having been bought with the revenue from my civil list, it will be suggested that the Senate decreed that the emperor's heirs could only inherit these after their value had exceeded thirty million francs; but that was for the future, it was a family ruling and one cannot suppose that I am not the owner of that furniture without doing me an injustice.
6. Laeken was bought with the revenues of the civil list, but the furnishings were paid for by revenues from my private estate; the sum in question comes to 800,000 francs, which should be demanded from the king of the Netherlands.
7. When the king of Sardinia and the grand duke of Tuscany were driven from their states in 1799 they took their silver, jewels and other valuables; they were even allowed to retain their private properties. What right do these rulers have to keep the silver and the furniture I sent to Paris, bought with the revenue of my civil list?
8. The pope removed his silver and valuables from Rome; the silver and the furniture which I sent to Rome was paid for from my civil list, and belongs to me by right.
9. I had a little farm on the island of Elba called *Saint-Martin,* valued at 200,000 francs with furnishings, carriages, carts, etc. It was bought with Princess Pauline's revenues. If it has been restored to her I am content; if not, my executors should ensure that restoration be effected to Princess Pauline if she is alive; if she is dead the farm is to form part of the sum total of my estate.
10. In Venice I had five millions of mercury which had, I think, been taken from the Austrians; to be followed up and recovered.
11. There are rumors concerning a will made by the patriarch of Venice; they are to be investigated.
12. Apart from all my books, I left at Malmaison two millions in gold and jewelry in a hiding place; no special gift was ever made to Empress Joséphine; I wish this sum to be drawn on only in so far as it is needed to fulfill my bequests.
13. I gave Empress Marie-Louise two millions in gold, in Orléans. She owes them to me, but I only wish this sum to be drawn on insofar as it is needed to fulfill my bequests.
14. I gave Denon and d'Albe a large number of plans belonging to me, since for several years I paid 10–20,000 francs a month in order to have such plans and designs made and drawn up; to be followed up and passed to my son.
15. I wish my executors to make a collection of engravings, pictures, books and medals which will give my son the right ideas and destroy any false ones which foreign politicians may inculate, in order that he will be in a position to see things as they really are. When printing the story of my Italian and Egyptian campaigns and those of my manuscripts which may be published, they and any letters from crowned heads that may be found are to be dedicated to my son. You should be able to get them out of the archives; it should not be difficult since national vanity will gain much from their publication.
16. If a collection of views of my headquarters, which used to be kept at Fontainebleau as well as the studies of my French and Italian palaces, could be assembled, it would make a fine collection for my son.
17. Constant stole a lot from me at Fontainebleau; I think that you could make him and Roustan surrender a lot of things which my son would find precious, but which have mere monetary value for them.
18. In my little apartments under the roof of the Tuileries there were a lot of chairs made by Joséphine and Marie-Louise, which my son might like.
19. When my executors shall be able to see my son they will make every effort to set his ideas right about facts and events, and put him back on the right path.

Instructions pour mes Exécuteurs Testamentaires

1° J'entends que mes legs soient payés dans leur intégrité.

2° Les 5,280,000 f que j'ai placé chez le banquier Laffitte doivent avoir produit au 1er Janvier 1821 d'intérêts étant comptés à 5 p. cent que je le lui ai dit environ 7,000,000 f en cas de difficulté il faut compter de chose moindre puisque des forces majeures m'ont empêché d'écrire et de disposer de mes fonds, je n'entends aucune modification la présente...

3° Je n'ai connaissance que le banquier Laffitte ait payé pour mon compte que 5, 20,000 au g. Vallancey ainsi ... doit, à Gillis mon valet de Chambre, 5, 100,000 ... Compte Lascazes, 5, 75,000 à Balcombe par une lettre de cr 3e de Comte Bertrand. Une autorisation envoyée par le Canal de Prince Eugène de fournir 12,000 f par mois depuis Roy a Londres pour mes besoins; somme ... si ce n'est une partie chez MM Parker à qui me vend redevable de sommes considérables au Cte Bertrand somme dont il doit tout d'abord être remboursé. D'où il résulte que le règlement de ce compte doit porter le fond que j'ai placé chez lui à la somme de 6,200,000 f Capital et intérêts en environ, disponibles, au 1er Janvier 1822.

4° La question de mon domaine privé est une question majeure, elle sera susceptible de beaucoup de débats, ...

5° Quand à tous les meubles de la Couronne qui m'appartiennent comme ayant été achetés des Deniers des ...

6° Lastrem a été acheté des Deniers du Domaine extraordinaire, ...

7° Lorsque le Roi de Sardaigne et le grand Duc de Toscane furent chassés de leurs états en 1777 ...

8° Le Pape a emporté de Rome son argenterie et ses objets précieux. L'argenterie et les meubles que j'ai ...

9° J'avais à l'Isle d'Elbe une petite maison appelée S. Martin estimé 200,000 f avec ...

10° J'avais à Nantes 5,000,000 f de mon argent qui m'ont été je crois en grande partie dérobés ...

11° Il court des bruits sur un testament de Patriarche de Venise, il faut bien approfondir.

12° J'avais laissé a Malmaison indépendamment de tous mes livres précieux en or et bijoux ...

13° J'ai donné à l'Impératrice Marie Louise 2,000,000 f en or à ordonné qu'elle me doit, ...

14° J'ai fait Dresde et d'Elbe une grande quantité de plans qui m'appartiennent ...

15° Je désire que mes exécuteurs testamentaires fassent une réunion de gravures, tableaux ...

16° Si on peut se procurer une collection de mes quartiers généraux qui étaient à Fontainebleau, ...

17° Constant m'a beaucoup volé à Fontainebleau je crois ...

18° Il y avait dans mes petits appartements un grand nombre de choses faites par Joséphine et Marie Louise ...

19° Quand mes exécuteurs testamentaires pourront voir mon fils ...

20. When they are able to see the empress (I wish this to happen in private and as soon as prudence permits) they will do so.

21. Without wishing my mother, if she be still alive, to single out my son in her will, since I imagine he will be richer than her other children, I would nevertheless like her to distinguish him with a few precious bequests, such as the portrait of my mother, or my father, or some jewels he can say he inherited from his grandparents.

22. As soon as my son has reached manhood, my mother, my brothers, my sisters must correspond with him and draw close to him, however much the house of Austria might oppose it, for the Austrians will then be powerless since my son will no longer be a minor.

23. I would be pleased to see officers or servants of mine entering into the service of my son, the children of Bertrand, of Montholon of, . . .

24. Instruct my son to re-adopt the name Napoleon as soon as he attains manhood and can do so with propriety.

25. Denon, d'Albe, Fain, Meveval, Bourrienne must have many things which would be of interest to my son.

26. When publishing my Italian memoirs use d'Albe for the plans. I had all the battlefields drawn up, and I think he has actually published them. The War Ministry will have the plans I made for several battles; I rather think that Jomini has them.

27. My executors must write to the king of England as they pass through England, to insist that my ashes be transported to France; they must write to the same effect to the French government.

28. If Las Cases assumes the office of treasurer, and my executors believe a secretary to be necessary and Drouot is agreeable, they may nominate him.

29. I have a little cousin in Ajaccio who owns, I think, some 300,000 francs' worth of land and is named Pallavicini. If she is not already married and Drouot likes her, her mother, knowing that such was my desire, will give her to him without

difficulty.

30. I wish my family to know that I desire my nephews and nieces to marry among themselves, either in the Roman states, or in the Swiss Republic or in the United States of America. I disapprove of marriages with Swedes, and, unless things change for the better in France, I want as little of my blood as possible at the court of their kings.

31. Appiani the Milanese painter will have many things of importance to my son; my memory shall be the glory of his life; assemble, acquire or make it possible for him to acquire everything which will contribute toward this aim.

32. If our luck changes and my son should mount the throne, it is the duty of my executors to draw his attention to everything that I owe to my old officers, men and faithful servants.

33. Write, and when possible tell Empress Marie-Louise of the constancy, the high regard and the feelings which I have entertained toward her, and constantly entrust my son to her keeping, for she is his sole resource.

34. If deputy Ramolino is in Paris, you can make use of him to find out about the state of my family, and how to correspond with it.

35. I wish my executors to obtain the drawings of myself which most resemble me, in various costumes, to send to my son as soon as they are able.

36. My wetnurse in Ajaccio had children and grandchildren which the situation I created for her enabled her to bring up in style. They will not be suspect to the Austrian authorities; try to place them in the service of my son. I imagine that she is dead. Anyway I think she is very rich; but if by some trick of fortune everything I did for her has failed to come right, my executors will not allow her to die in poverty.

37. I would not be displeased if little Léon were to enter the judiciary, if that appeals to him. I would like Alexander Walewski to enter the service of France as a soldier.

NAPOLEON

20° ...

21° ...

22° ...

23° ...

24° ...

25° ...

26° ...

27° ...

28° ...

29° ...

30° ...

31° ...

32° ...

33° ...

34° ...

35° ...

36° ...

37° ...

Annexé par Nous, notaire
à Paris, soussigné, à la
minute d'un Artificat
de Dépôt dressé par
Nous aujourd'hui sept
juillet mil huit cent
cinquante-trois.

Signé et paraphé au dessus de
notre procès-verbal de ce jour.
Paris le vingt trois juin 1853

These are some instructions for Montholon, Bertrand and Marchand, my executors.

I have made a will with seven codicils, leaving it with Marchand.

NAPOLEON

April 27.

Ceci est une instr...
pour Mathioter. Bertaud
et Marchand ? ...
exécuteures testamentai...
j'ai fait testament
en ... rendicter dom
marchand est
de pontane
le 29 avril ...

Napoleon as emperor of the French, 1804. From the coronation painting by David.

Napoleon as captive of the English, on board H.M.S. *Bellerophon*.
From the painting by W. Q. Orchardson.

NAPOLEON BUONAPARTE,

*from a Drawing taken by Capt.ⁿ Dodgin of the 66.ᵗʰ Regiment
at S.ᵗ Helena during 1820.*

The son and heir, Napoleon II. "I urge him never to forget that he was born a French prince . . ." He died an Austrian duke.

Lady Holland, who for the kindness she showed Napoleon during his exile was to receive "the antique cameo which Pope Pius VI gave me in Tolentino."

Sir Hudson Lowe, governor of St. Helena, was bequeathed the lasting reputation of clerk, hangman and "hired assassin."

Trappings of empire: One of Napoleon's ceremonial robes, typifying the deliberate splendor of the imperial image.

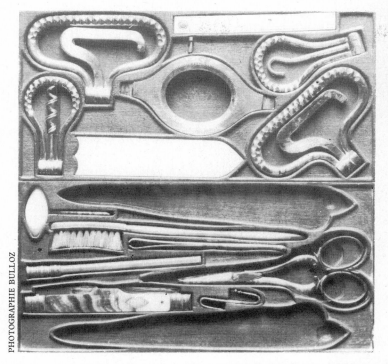

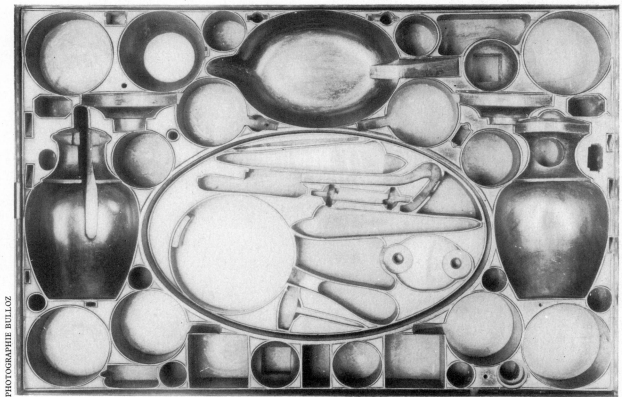

Trappings of war: utensils Napoleon used in the field, in their exquisitely crafted cases.

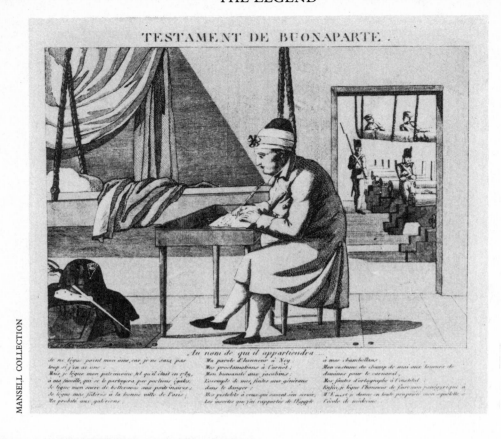

This satirical anti-Bonapartist cartoon shows
Napoleon writing his will, in which he
bequeathes his integrity to galley-slaves, his
humanity to the Jacobins and a uniform to the
hirers of carnival costumes.

A different view: the will strove to perpetuate
the Napoleonic legend, whose power and
romance influenced this depiction of the
emperor on his deathbed.